How to Pass

SECOND EDITION

HIGHER

Administration & IT

Anne Bradley
and Adam Stephenson

HODDER GIBSON

AN HACHETTE UK COMPANY

The Publishers would like to thank the following for permission to reproduce copyright material:

Photo credits

p.2 © Keith Bell/123RF; **p.5** © Ganna Rassadnikova/123RF; **p.6** © andrewgenn/iStock/Thinkstock; **p.10** © marigranula/123RF; **p.14** © Zerbor/stock.adobe.com; **p.29** © Askold Romanov/iStock/Thinkstock **p.30** © Photodisc/Getty Images/World Commerce & Travel 5; **p.31** © vinnstock/istock/ Thinkstock; **p.33** © Yuriy Kirsanov/123; **p.35** Screenshot used with kind permission of TripAdvisor; **p.37** © litu92458/iStock/Thinkstock; **p.38** © Hodder Education; **p.40** © 2015 Google Inc, used with permission. Google and Google logo are registered trademarks of Google Inc; **p.41** Screenshot used with kind permission of SCHOLAR, Heriot-Watt University © 2015; **p.42** © kasto/123RF; **p.45** © AVAVA – Fotolia.com; **p.88** © Stepan Popov /123RF

Screenshots from Microsoft products are used with permission from Microsoft.

Acknowledgements

Understanding Standards tables on pages 150–1 adapted from sources available on SQA's website by kind permission, copyright © Scottish Qualifications Authority. Keynote is a trademark of Apple Inc. Access, PowerPoint, Microsoft, Lync, Excel and Skype are either registered trademarks of Microsoft Corporation in the United States and/or other countries.

Every effort has been made to trace all copyright holders, but if any have been inadvertently overlooked, the Publishers will be pleased to make the necessary arrangements at the first opportunity.

Although every effort has been made to ensure that website addresses are correct at time of going to press, Hodder Gibson cannot be held responsible for the content of any website mentioned in this book. It is sometimes possible to find a relocated web page by typing in the address of the home page for a website in the URL window of your browser.

Hachette UK's policy is to use papers that are natural, renewable and recyclable products and made from wood grown in well-managed forests and other controlled sources. The logging and manufacturing processes are expected to conform to the environmental regulations of the country of origin.

Orders: please contact Bookpoint Ltd, 130 Park Drive, Milton Park, Abingdon, Oxon OX14 4SE. Telephone: (44) 01235 827827. Fax: (44) 01235 400454. Email education@bookpoint.co.uk Lines are open from 9 a.m. to 5 p.m., Monday to Friday, with a 24-hour message answering service. Visit our website at www.hoddereducation.co.uk. If you have queries or questions that aren't about an order, you can contact us at hoddergibson@hodder.co.uk

SCOTLAND EXCEL

We are an approved supplier on the Scotland Excel framework.

Schools can find us on their procurement system as: **Hodder & Stoughton Limited t/a Hodder Gibson.**

First published in 2019 by
Hodder Gibson, an imprint of Hodder Education
An Hachette UK Company
211 St Vincent Street
Glasgow, G2 5QY

Impression number   5   4   3
Year   2023 2022 2021 2020

Cover photo © Maksym – stock.adobe.com
Illustrations by Aptara, Inc
Typeset in Cronus Pro Light 13/15pt. by Aptara, Inc.
Printed in India
A catalogue record for this title is available from the British Library
ISBN: 978 1 5104 5223 7

MIX
Paper from responsible sources
FSC™ C104740
FSC
www.fsc.org

Contents

Introduction

Welcome to *How to Pass Higher Administration and IT*. This book has been written specifically to prepare you for the **Higher Administration and IT** course. It will help you to prepare for the Coursework: IT Assignment and Question Paper. This book is intended for use in the classroom by students and teachers alike; however, it can also be used to supplement the work done by you in school or college when preparing/revising for ongoing and Course Assessments.

How to use this book

The book contains some features that will help you to make the most of your study of Administration and IT. They are:

What you should know

These sections are there to emphasise the learning outcomes that *you must know* so that you can demonstrate enough knowledge and understanding to easily meet the standard required for all areas of the course as set by the SQA. You will be assessed on these areas in the course assessment.

Remember

This feature provides examiners' advice on what key terms to remember, and how. It also suggests what you need to do to gain the maximum marks available in your final course assessment.

Activity

An activity will help you to apply your skills, knowledge and understanding of a topic.

Exam-style questions practice

These questions will reflect the type of questions which appear in the external question paper.

Note

Extra information and useful pointers.

Hints & tips

This feature gives you extra information to help you achieve top marks and common mistakes to avoid.

E-files

E-files are available to download, free of charge, to assist in the completion of the practice assignment and word processing/spreadsheet /database examples. The e-files can be accessed via the Updates and Extras section of the Hodder Gibson pages at www.hoddereducation.co.uk, but it should be noted that, in line with the aims and objectives of the course, specific solutions are not provided.

The course

The Higher Administration and IT course is split into two areas:

- Administrative theory and practice
- IT applications.

This book has seven main chapters which cover the knowledge and understanding and the mandatory skills required for each component.

Course assessment

The course assessment for Higher Administration and IT is made up of two components: a written question paper and an IT-based assignment.

Component one: question paper

The question paper is set by SQA and will be done during the main examination diet. The exam is *closed book* – which means you won't have access to notes or books. It is designed to give you the opportunity to show the examiner that you can apply your knowledge and understanding of administrative theory from all aspects of the course and draw valid conclusions on evidence provided.

The question paper has two sections to be completed within a time limit of **1 hour 30 minutes**.

Section 1 (10 marks): this will consist of some information in the form of a 'case study' (known as stimulus material) and a set of mandatory questions (*this means you have to answer ALL of them*), each worth between 1 and 6 marks. The questions are based on the information provided in the case study and on the knowledge and understanding you have gained while studying the course.

Section 2 (40 marks): this section will also be made up of mandatory questions based on all sections of the course (each worth between 1 and 6 marks) – this ensures that the question paper gives a balanced coverage across the course.

Command words

Command words are used in each question in the Question Paper. The command word is the FIRST word of the question and is there to help you answer the question in the way it is expected.

> *Hints & tips* ⭐
>
> *A command word is not a polite request to do something – you must attempt to word your answer in the required manner.*

Below is a list of the common command words used in Higher Administration and IT questions with some hints on the best way to answer them.

Command word	Explanation	Hints on how to answer
Outline	Give a number of brief statements which might be facts, features or characteristics.	Keep your answers short. You won't receive any marks for expanding your answers in an outline, so keep it short and simple.
Justify	Give a good reason to support a course of action or suggestion.	Try to explain the reason for or against an issue raised by the question being asked. (It is more likely to be an advantage of a suggestion or course of action, rather than a disadvantage.)
Describe	Make a number of relevant factual points – features and/or characteristics (relating to a process, concept or situation).	This can be a number of straightforward points or a smaller number of developed points (or a combination of both) including examples where appropriate.
Explain	Make points that relate cause and effect and/or make the relationships clear – (relating to a process, concept or situation).	This can be a number of straightforward points of explanation or a smaller number of developed points (or a combination of both) including examples where appropriate. Make use of link phrases, e.g. 'this means', 'which will', 'therefore', when explaining the effect of the cause – and 'because', 'as this' when explaining the cause as related to the effect.
Discuss	Communicate ideas and information on a subject in a structured manner.	More than naming – there must be an element of discussion within each point – sometimes used to illustrate the case for or against an idea. Make use of link phrases, e.g. 'however', 'but', 'or' within any statements being made.
Compare	Make points that **clearly** show knowledge and understanding of the similarities and/or differences between things, features, methods or choices.	Only one mark per point of comparison (in effect two points for one mark). Make use of link phrases, e.g. 'both' to illustrate similarities and 'whereas', 'however', 'but', 'on the other hand' to illustrate differences. Points of comparison must be related – not just two random points.

Exam questions

You need to practise using command words by answering as many past paper questions (old and new) as you can.

You should try to identify the differences between what appear to be similar questions – i.e. the same topic but using a different command word. This should help you understand the quantity and quality of writing needed to gain full marks.

It is also important that you read the question carefully – I know you have heard this many times but it is easy to skim over a question when in an examination situation.

Remember

Take care using solutions to past paper questions – they tend to only give basic facts/ statements relating to the question regardless of the command word.

Exam-style questions (example) ⊚

Explain the importance of effective file management on the intranet. **(3 marks)**

Suggested answer

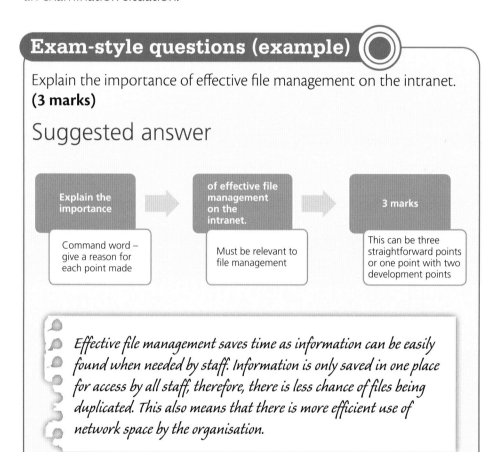

Effective file management saves time as information can be easily found when needed by staff. Information is only saved in one place for access by all staff, therefore, there is less chance of files being duplicated. This also means that there is more efficient use of network space by the organisation.

Comments from marker

The first sentence is a straightforward and valid point and would be awarded one mark. The second sentence is another valid point and the third sentence is a development point (re information being in one place). This response would gain the full three marks available.

Note the use of link words – *'as'*, *'therefore'* and *'also means'*. More importantly, the question has not been repeated three times – never a good idea.

Component two: assignment

This assignment is worth **70 marks** (58 per cent of the overall mark) and will be completed by you in school or college under a high degree of supervision and control over a single **2-hour** time period. Evidence of the completed task will be printed and submitted to the SQA by the due date for marking.

The assessment will assess your skills, knowledge and understanding as follows:

- The use of complex IT functions in word processing, spreadsheets, databases, desktop publishing , e-diary and presentation software to produce, process, manage information and solve problems.
- The use of electronic research to source and effectively communicate complex information.
- To display a wide range of administrative and problem-solving skills related to the administrative function viz planning and organising.

The assignment requires you to apply skills and knowledge of IT applications to produce, manage and analyse information and to solve problems.

Marks will be awarded for demonstrating skills in the use of the different IT applications as follows.

Task	Mark allocation
Spreadsheet / Database / Word Processing	20 marks will be allocated to each of these areas, with a variance of (plus or minus) 4 marks in each area
Communication (e.g. presentation, email, e-diary, internet)	10 marks will be allocated with a variance of (plus or minus) 2 marks
TOTAL	**70 marks**

Hints & tips

Original printouts of your IT tasks must show your name and centre clearly displayed on each printout but they must be typed, not handwritten.

Remember

You can only be awarded marks for evidence submitted — make sure you print ALL evidence requested in the task — COUNT and CHECK!

Finally

Revise, revise, revise your notes! There are many books with tips on how to revise effectively, but really it is down to you to go over ALL areas of the Administrative Theory and Practice and learn by whatever method suits you – mind maps, flash cards, etc. However, if you are aware of the meaning of the command words and what is expected of you, and you practise how to answer them properly, it will become second nature to you and all you have to do is fill in the blanks!

Practise, practise, practise your IT skills Become an expert! There are lots of exercises based on the functions of the software you use – if you know how to do them (quickly and efficiently) by repeating them over and over, again it will become second nature to you and all you have to do is input the data!

Make your examiner smile When he/she opens your script/printouts and recognises evidence of hard work and proper preparation when marking your exam paper, you know it makes sense!

> Please see *National 4 & 5 Administration and IT* by Anne Bradley and Adam Stephenson, if looking to revise any of the topics covered in this book.

Component 1 Administrative theory and practice

Chapter 1

Factors contributing to the effectiveness of the administrative practices within an organisation

What you should know

There are **six** topics to this chapter. By the end of this chapter you should be able to:

1 Understand the role of Administrative and Senior Administrative Assistants.
2 Describe strategies for effective time and task management and their importance.
3 Describe the characteristics of effective teams.
4 Explain strategies to ensure compliance with workplace legislation.
5 Describe the appropriate steps to manage information and how to maintain security and confidentiality.
6 Explain the impact of modern IT on working practices.

1 Administrative and Senior Administrative Assistants

An Administrative Assistant helps with the smooth running of an organisation's office and handles basic clerical duties. Often an Administrative Assistant will progress to become a Senior Administrative Assistant, at which point assisting company managers is added to the role. Generally, the duties of these two professionals are virtually the same, but the Senior Administrative Assistant typically takes on more responsibility than the Administrative Assistant.

Both the Senior Administrative Assistant and Administrative Assistant are likely to work with office software (word processing, database, spreadsheet, presentation and email programs) and associated hardware. The training of new staff members may also be a duty of both these professionals. However, there are certain responsibilities that distinguish one from the other.

Administrative Assistant	Senior Administrative Assistant
● Carries out routine tasks delegated by the Senior Administrative Assistant	● Does the type of work more concentrated on attending to the needs of managers
● Enters/updates business data into a database or spreadsheet ● Maintains documents and files	● May also be given the authority to supervise other staff in the office, overseeing their tasks
● Assists with scheduling meetings ● Sends emails to colleagues ● Prepares documentation for meetings	● Often prepares reports and presentations for managers to use or delegates these tasks to an Administrative Assistant
● Greets and directs visitors ● Deals with answering incoming calls	● Is responsible for managing the daily schedule and setting up personal appointments for one or more high-level managers in a company

Senior Administrative Assistants are called upon to do duties that require greater sensitivity and therefore generally have more experience than an Administrative Assistant. Both the Administrative and the Senior Administrative Assistant offer advanced administrative support for managers and heads of department. What separates their jobs from other positions that involve more routine and clerical tasks is the level of **confidentiality** and **responsibility** that is required.

Exam-style questions practice

1 Compare the duties of the Administrative Assistant with those of the Senior Administrative Assistant. (3 marks)

2 Time and task management

The definition of time management is given as 'the ability to use one's time effectively or productively, especially at work' and task management can be defined as 'finishing an assigned piece of work in a certain amount of time'.

Generally speaking, this means developing procedures and tools that increase efficiency and productivity in the workplace. This sounds simple, but it can become a problem that has to be addressed in many modern workplaces.

Why?

When trying to manage time we realise we only have a certain amount of time available yet the number of tasks seems to be ever-increasing. In other words, no matter how organised we appear to be there are still only 24 hours in a day! Therefore, *time and task management skills* are essential for any administrator who can find themselves performing a great variety of tasks during the working day.

Remember

A skill is something that you can learn and become better at with practice.

These *skills* can be broken down into stages as follows:

- planning
- delegating
- organising
- directing/controlling.

Collectively these are known as *organising strategies*. It can seem to be daunting to be good at all of these, but to be effective it is best to break them down into steps.

Planning

Whether it is a special event (e.g. a promotional launch event, special presentation) or regular events (monthly management meetings, business trips, file management) it is important to plan ahead.

Creating a to-do list, action plan or a priorities list are the most obvious methods as this will help to identify individual tasks that need to be done and, perhaps even more importantly, the order they need to be done in to effectively overtake the demands of the completed task.

What is a to-do list?

This is a list of all the tasks that need to be carried out over a period of time. They list everything that you have to do, in the order that they need to be done. Organising your tasks with a list can make everything much more manageable and will help you feel organised and stay focused.

As you cross items off your to-do list, you will feel a sense of progress and accomplishment that can be missed when rushing from one activity to the next. The knowledge that you are making progress will help motivate you to keep moving forward rather than feeling overwhelmed.

What is an action plan?

An action plan is a document that lists what steps must be taken in order to achieve a specific target or goal. The purpose of an action plan is to clearly identify what resources are required and the timescale needed to complete specific tasks.

A well-developed action plan identifies the tasks to be done and who is responsible for completing them. It allows a complex task to be broken down into smaller, more manageable SMART targets.

S – Specific – exactly what has to be done – well defined.

M – Measurable – how much has to be done – know when it has been achieved.

A – Attainable/Agreed – should be acceptable to all.

R – Realistic – be within your capability and have the resources available.

T – Time-based – has a start and end date – enough to complete the task.

To make these lists or plans more effective it is important that they are prioritised – some tasks are important and some are urgent – some are both!

What is a priorities list?

All daily work needs clear priorities – time is always limited and so one of the biggest challenges for an Administrative Assistant is to prioritise work accurately on a daily basis.

The following steps can be used to prioritise workload:

1 **Collect a list of all your tasks.** Review your **to-do list**. At this stage, the order or number of items is not important.

2 **Identify what is urgent and what is important.** See if you have any tasks that need immediate attention, i.e. work that if not completed by the end of the day or in the next few hours will have serious negative consequences (*for example, a missed client deadline, a missed publication or release deadline*).

3 **Assess value.** Look at your important work and identify what carries the highest value to the organisation. In general, it is important to recognise exactly which types of tasks have priority over others, for example, focusing on client projects **before** internal work.

   Another way to assess value is to look at how many people are affected by your work. In general, the **more people involved**, the higher the priority.

4 **Order tasks by estimated effort.** If you have tasks that seem to have the same priority, think about starting on whichever one you think will take the most effort to complete. **But**, if you feel you can't focus on more difficult work, then it can be motivating to check a small task off the list first.

5 **Be flexible and adaptable.** Uncertainty and change are always a possibility. Know that priorities can change, often when least expected. It is important, however, to stay focused on the tasks you are committed to completing.

6 **Be realistic and know when to cut tasks from the list.** You probably can't get to everything on the list.

   After you prioritise your tasks and look at your time estimates, cut some tasks from the list, and focus on the priorities that you know **you must and can complete** during the day.

Example

Monica is sitting at her desk using the time she allocated in her diary for file management – making sure all the files and folders that have been sitting on her computer desktop are put into appropriate locations on the organisation's server. After just 5 minutes the phone rings and, of course, she answers it. It is an automated voice telling her that she could be eligible for compensation for having been mis-sold insurance. She is a bit annoyed and decides to continue with her work and to ignore her ringing phone.

Some emails pop-up while she is working and she opens her email program – to discover it is a funny email. She is amused and reads the email. She decides to check her social media page while online, returning to her file management task after some time has elapsed. She is now behind in her work and has to miss her scheduled morning break to catch up.

To get on top of her workload Monica tries to write some emails while she chats on the phone to her customers. Her customers are frustrated by her lack of attention and her emails are full of typos and errors!

What was urgent and what was important?

✔ Answering the phone is urgent: if you ignore it the caller may ring off and you will not know why they called. However, it may not be important.

✔ Doing regular file management tasks is important. It is not initially urgent but, if left too long, it may become more pressing because you will be unable to locate files or other related problems.

✘ Reading funny emails or checking social media is neither urgent nor important – it is a distraction which needs to be minimised – *more on that later*.

✔ Scheduled breaks provide valuable downtime – enabling more effective work to be achieved.

✔ Urgent tasks demand immediate attention – but whether they are done may or may not matter. *Important tasks matter – not doing them will have consequences.* If the task is important but time is short, then delegating the task should be considered.

and finally,

✘ Although Monica thinks she is making good use of her time, in truth she is probably taking more time to finish her workload while multi-tasking compared with completing the same tasks in an orderly way. It is better to focus on one task at a time – producing higher quality work.

Hints & tips ★

In order to achieve good time and task management it is important to understand the difference between Urgent and Important!

Delegating

Once tasks have been broken down into steps by the action plan or to-do list, it will be easier for the Senior Administrative Assistant to consider whether any can be delegated to an Administrative Assistant. It is important to remember that it can sometimes take longer to delegate a task (because it is complicated to explain) than to do it! However, if the task is easy to explain – but time-consuming to do – it is a perfect task for delegation.

Once a task/event has been broken down into logical steps/parts, effective delegation can happen by considering the following:

- Does the whole task need to be done straight away?
- Do all of the parts of the task need to be done immediately?
- Can they be done by someone else easily and effectively?

Although delegation is a good idea to ensure that deadlines are met, it is important to be aware of the level of control needed over a task. It is important to find the correct balance between *micromanaging* on the one hand and trusting others to do a task with the minimum direction.

Delegation is a *skill* – failure to develop this skill can result in making the mistake of taking on too much work. This can lead to poor quality work, stress and low morale. *See Benefits and Consequences table (page 9).*

"Maybe we are micro-managing a bit too much."

> **Note** !
>
> A micromanager is a manager who insists on controlling or doing all of the work themselves!

Organising

Being organised doesn't happen by accident or chance. It is a good idea to schedule time in your diary – *first thing in the morning or last thing at the end of the working day* – to think about what needs to be done that day or the next. Taking time on a regular basis to think about what has to be done and when – especially those tasks with time-limits or deadlines – will mean less stress in the workplace.

Keeping tidy helps with being organised in the workplace. It is easier to stay on top of things if your workstation is tidy. If everything is on your desk or computer desktop, then it is impossible to prioritise what needs action, what doesn't and what has been actioned. Having a place for everything and everything in its place means that you will be able to see at a glance what needs doing.

Keep	Save or give away	Archive or delete
If you need a particular document or file for your records, file it in an appropriate place in your personal work area. If you need to do something with a document or file – add it to your task list.	If a document or file is not required by you but someone else may need it, put it on the server or give it to the person who needs it.	Any documents or files that have some value but are not needed often – or are of no further use to the business – should be deleted completely to free up space on the server.

Directing and controlling

A properly thought out action plan helps break large-scale events or tasks down into manageable steps, making it easy to see everything that needs to get done, when it needs to be done, and so can be completed in small pieces at a time – and by more than one person through delegation.

There are various methods which could be used to monitor and evaluate the progress of delegated work.

Method	Example
Review meetings	A manager can carry out periodic checks on progress by meeting with the member(s) of staff on a regular basis to ensure progress is being made as scheduled and can offer support and advice when required.
Mentoring	A more senior member of staff can be assigned to a junior member of staff to oversee the task as it is completed. This would ensure that any problems could be addressed immediately and would allow the junior employee to complete the task with less stress.
Buddy system	Similar to mentoring, except that the member of staff would be at the same level. The Buddy would have more experience and be familiar with all the details of the job and be available for help and advice.
Appraisal	This is where meetings take place to review performance and helps to identify any training and development required by staff. This can also help assess the member of staff's career development.
Personal Development Plan	This is where an employee sets their own targets for future skills development. These targets would match with those of the organisation/department. Having a personal development plan helps you make sure your knowledge, skills and abilities are constantly upgraded.

Controlling and monitoring work and workflow can be achieved by setting targets for individual members of staff and the organisation as a whole. Once a target or goal is set, it can be easily measured against work achieved. This can be done using strategies such as updating and reviewing action plans and to-do lists regularly.

Gantt charts can also be used to check progress – especially if it is a large-scale event or project that is being organised.

What is a Gantt chart?

A Gantt chart shows tasks or events displayed against a time limit. It consists of a list of the tasks to be done (usually displayed down the left-hand side) and along the top is a suitable timescale – e.g. days, weeks and months. Each activity is represented by a bar; the position and length of the bar reflects the start date, length of time planned and an end date of the activity.

This allows you to see at a glance:
- What the various tasks are.
- When each task begins and ends.
- How long each task is scheduled to last.
- Where tasks overlap with other tasks, and by how much.
- The start and end date of the whole project.

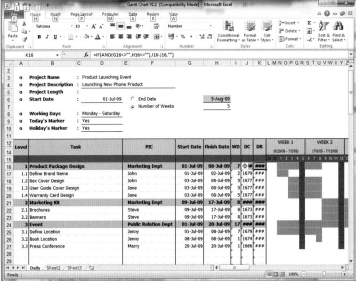

To summarise, a Gantt chart shows you what has to be done (the tasks) and when (time-scale). Gantt charts can be easily created and updated using a special software package such as MindView - Gantt Chart Software ®.

Exam-style questions practice

2 Outline four methods which a Senior Administrative Assistant could use to monitor an employee's work. (4 marks)

3 Describe three time management strategies a Senior Administrative Assistant could use to be more effective in the workplace. (6 marks)

4 Justify the need for a Senior Administrative Assistant to monitor and evaluate a Junior Administrative Assistant's work. (3 marks)

Dealing with changes in priorities

This a problem that everyone faces at some point or another, and while it is difficult to skilfully juggle changing priorities and competing responsibilities, it is not impossible. In order for a time management process to work it is important to know what aspects of our personal management need to be improved. Unexpected problems can disrupt even the most carefully organised schedule. Problems will always develop, so plan for them. Set aside some time each day to deal with unexpected issues – if nothing develops, you'll have the benefit of extra time to complete other work or enjoy a short break.

Below you will find some of the most frequent distractions responsible for reducing effectiveness in the workplace. These are commonly known as time stealers. Fortunately there are strategies you can use to manage your time in a better way, be more in control and reduce stress.

Procrastination

If you have identified a task as both important and urgent, and you still keep putting it off, that is procrastination. Sometimes it is because you are unsure of how to do a task or it is an unpleasant task. Once you've decided that you really do need to do something, there are plenty of things that you can do to help you avoid procrastinating. Minimising distractions is the best way forward.

Important task	Suggested strategies to manage distractions
Phone	When making or receiving a call: be polite, listen and clarify but try to avoid excessive small talk, keeping calls as brief as possible.
	Use voicemail wisely and set aside times to return missed calls.
	Have a personal mobile phone – friends and family can then still reach you in an emergency.
Email	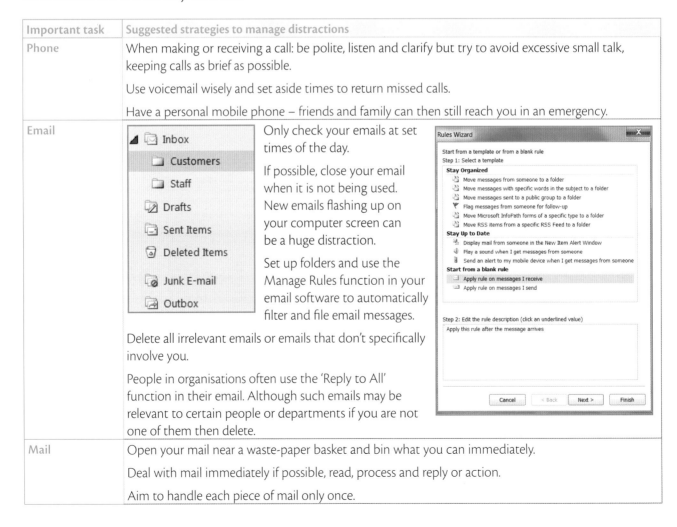 Only check your emails at set times of the day. If possible, close your email when it is not being used. New emails flashing up on your computer screen can be a huge distraction. Set up folders and use the Manage Rules function in your email software to automatically filter and file email messages.
	Delete all irrelevant emails or emails that don't specifically involve you.
	People in organisations often use the 'Reply to All' function in their email. Although such emails may be relevant to certain people or departments if you are not one of them then delete.
Mail	Open your mail near a waste-paper basket and bin what you can immediately.
	Deal with mail immediately if possible, read, process and reply or action.
	Aim to handle each piece of mail only once.

Important task	Suggested strategies to manage distractions
Computers	Close programs and documents when you have finished using them – file your documents in a logical way.
	Close web pages after you have finished reading them. This is especially important for news or social networking sites where information is updated constantly.
Unexpected visitors/meetings	Try to avoid being interrupted – be firm with colleagues who just want to chat.
	Let people know when you are available to meet and refer to these as appointments. The word 'appointment' is more formal and people are more likely to come for a specific reason. If visitors arrive at an inconvenient time then politely explain that you cannot see them and reschedule.

Managing time effectively can improve productivity – but it is not possible to focus and produce high-quality work without taking a break. It is not a waste of time. Breaks provide valuable downtime to enable more creative and effective work to happen!

	Benefits of good time and task management
Using To-Do lists and/or Action Plan	✓ Deadlines are met ✓ Greater productivity ✓ Better quality of work ✓ Staff have more control of workload ✓ Less stress on staff ✓ Targets are achieved The most effective To-Do List should always include a system of prioritising tasks on the list. Also, large tasks should be broken down into specific, attainable steps – to avoid vague and ineffective entries on the list.
Good file management/ organised desk	✓ Information found when required ✓ Information can be found by others
Delegation	✓ Staff more motivated ✓ Staff feel empowered ✓ Deadlines are met
	Consequences of bad time and task management
Taking on too much	✗ Can lead to stress as a result of heavy workload ✗ Can result in illness/absenteeism ✗ Poor performance leading to poor-quality work ✗ Deadlines missed
Failure to delegate	✗ Lack of trust within a team leading to low staff morale within a department ✗ Staff unable to deputise for the manager when required

Exam-style questions practice

5 Outline the reasons why a Senior Administrative Assistant may be reluctant to delegate a task. (2 marks)
6 Describe the long-term implications for a Senior Administrative Assistant who fails to delegate tasks to a Junior Administrative Assistant. (6 marks)
7 Describe strategies which could be used to overcome the problem caused by **two** common time stealers. (4 marks)

3 Effective teams

Features of an effective team

> 'A team is not a bunch of people with job titles, but a congregation of individuals, each of whom has a role which is understood by other members.'
> *Dr R Meredith Belbin*

A team is usually put together for a specific purpose and each team member should be chosen to ensure that the correct balance of skill is achieved.

An effective team is normally small – realistically between four and six people. Too many can cause management problems resulting in an ineffective team. Too few could mean that there is not enough experience and or skills to make the team effective.

A good team also requires a good team leader who can create the conditions that allow ideas and people to work well together, to empower them and create a good working atmosphere.

Good teamwork doesn't just happen. Conscious effort is needed to help groups of individuals work together as a team. Good team performance and positive team relations need to be developed and maintained. Individual members of a team must exhibit certain skills/qualities.

- **Co-operation:** active participation and willing co-operation earns the respect of other team members, making them more willing to share ideas.
- **Listening:** showing support to others when they speak fosters an environment which allows sharing and debate about ideas and solutions to take place.
- **Responsibility:** to achieve success it is important that each team member accepts responsibility for completion of their allotted task and takes responsibility for any errors.

What makes a team effective?	
Presence of a good leader	Helps to promote positive atmosphere/good staff morale.
	Provides good communication channels.
	Helps ensure deadlines are met through effective monitoring.
	Allows management of all types of people to avoid conflict within a team.
Open and transparent communication	Values other team members' contributions to be heard without prejudice.
	Allows team members to express themselves avoiding frustration and conflict.
	Enables new ideas to be brought in.
	Encourages team members to compromise where necessary.

What makes a team effective?	
Good mix of skills and personalities	• Being responsible for tasks allocated.
	• Helpful and supportive to other members of the team.
	• Leads to better productivity.
Shared knowledge/skills	• Allows work to progress smoothly in times of absence whether work-related or through illness.
Good training available	• Gives team leader and/or members of the team confidence in their ability.
	• Helps to support completion of challenging tasks.
Clear purpose/goal	• Helps to have a common direction – encouraging co-operation within the team.
	• Helps to create a productive environment.

Activity

Visit the Belbin Website (www.belbin.com) where you can find out more about what makes an effective team and the roles within an effective team. Watch the presentation on the home page:

"A guide to Belbin Team Roles"

• Take any notes that might help you study and understand this topic later.
• Download and save and/or print the pdf file, 'Team Roles in a Nutshell'. Keep this information in among your notes and tasks for Effective Teams.

Benefits of effective teamwork

	Benefit
To the organisation	• Better ideas generated which makes the organisation more productive and competitive.
	• Communication between staff in the organisation is improved if they are working in teams.
	• Can reduce staff turnover and/or staff absence as individual employees are often motivated by being part of a team.
	• Motivated and happy staff can help reduce the cost of recruitment and/or training.
	• Employees can develop skills more confidently, increasing flexibility if someone is absent.
To the employee	• Will feel more supported in the workplace.
	• Can learn more skills from other members of the team.
	• Greater job satisfaction as they can confidently complete set tasks.
	• Will become more experienced.
	• Leads to employees being more motivated and less likely to be stressed.
	• May increase chances of promotion.
	• May lead to higher pay/bonuses if meeting targets.

Exam-style questions practice

8 An effective leader should have 'good people skills'. Outline **four** other leadership skills you would expect to see in an effective leader. (4 marks)

9 Describe **three** ways in which a team may be affected by a poor team leader. (6 marks)

10 Good teamwork is essential for efficiency and productivity. Discuss reasons why some teams are more effective than others. (6 marks)

4 Workplace regulations

Health and safety legislation

Most organisations are required to have a written policy on health and safety which must be available to all staff.

Health and safety within the workplace is the responsibility of both the employer and employee. It is important that health and safety is seen as an integral part of good business practice. Good health and safety practices and support are a tangible way that the employer uses to show how highly they value their employees. At the same time the employees' role in the system is to take responsibility for themselves and their co-workers, to do their jobs well and safely, and to observe and monitor their working environment. Health and safety should not be seen as something separate but should be regarded as a safety culture rather than simple compliance.

The Health and Safety at Work etc Act 1974 (also referred to as HSWA, the HSW Act, the 1974 Act or HASAWA) is the primary piece of legislation covering occupational health and safety in Great Britain.

Activity

- Visit the Health and Safety Executive website (**www.hse.gov. uk/legislation**) where you can find out the most up-to-date information on legislation today. Click on the link to the Health and Safety at Work Act.
- Scroll down this page and download and save and/or print the pdf file – 'Health and safety made simple'. *If printing – use booklet style and back-to-back option (duplex).*
- Next download and save and/or print the pdf file – 'Health and safety law' – leaflet OR pocket size (you decide).

Health and safety laws apply to all organisations and are there to protect the employer, employee and visitors from workplace dangers. The approach taken by all organisations to health and safety should be proportionate to the size and nature of the business activity. If there are fewer than five employees there is no need to write down a health and safety policy.

Note

It is important to think about homeworkers and others (e.g. visitors) who may not be in the workplace all of the time!

Responsibilities for health and safety

The employer must provide all employees with:

✓ training to enable work to be done safely
✓ any equipment and protection necessary
✓ health checks (if work requires).

Employer	Responsibility
Welfare – must provide:	<ul><li>toilets and hand basins, with soap, towels and hand-dryer</li><li>drinking water</li><li>a place to store clothing</li><li>somewhere to rest and eat meals.</li></ul>
Health – make sure there is:	<ul><li>good ventilation</li><li>a reasonable temperature (in offices at least 16°C)</li><li>suitable lighting</li><li>enough space and suitable workstations and seating</li><li>a clean workplace with appropriate waste containers.</li></ul>
Safety – to keep the workplace safe there must be:	<ul><li>properly maintained premises and work equipment</li><li>floors free from obstructions</li><li>windows that can be opened and cleaned safely</li><li>safety glass or suitably protected material on all doors and walls.</li></ul>
First aid arrangements in place (minimum)	<ul><li>suitably stocked first aid box</li><li>an appropriate person to take charge of first aid</li><li>first aid information available for all employees</li><li>if more than ten employees, there must be an Accident Book (under social security law).</li></ul>
Training must be provided:	<ul><li>for current and proposed working practices</li><li>for any new employees or employees who change their job.</li></ul>
Finally	A Health and Safety law poster must be displayed OR each employee must have a copy (leaflet or pocket size). This must be the revised version – published in 2009.

Employees must:
- take care of their own health and safety
- take care of the health and safety of people who work around them
- co-operate with others on health and safety and not interfere with, or misuse, anything provided for health and safety or welfare
- follow training given.

Health and Safety (First Aid) Regulations 1981

The First Aid Regulations require all employers, even small businesses, and the self-employed to make sure that there are appropriate facilities, equipment and appointed personnel to give employees immediate attention should they be injured in the workplace.

Interestingly, there is no legal requirement under the Act for organisations to make provision for any non-employees – which would include customers or even students in a school; however, the regulations make recommendations that these groups are provided for when planning first aid provision.

As a bare minimum, all organisations are required to have:
- a suitably stocked first aid kit
- an appointed person to take charge of first aid arrangements
- information for employees about first aid arrangements.

Employers are required to assess the risk in the workplace and provide appropriate provision – there are no set stipulations in the regulations as every workplace is different and employers are the people best placed to decide what is necessary. For example, an organisation that is largely office based, with staff mainly answering calls and using computers, would be low risk compared to a factory where staff may be using chemicals or heavy machinery. These two types of organisations would have different first aid equipment on site and train their staff to deal with different types of medical situations – the factory would probably have a number of staff trained in first aid and the office may decide they do not need anyone to be trained in first aid.

First aid box

Provision for first aid is at the discretion of the employer, based on their risk assessment. The Health and Safety Executive (HSE) provide a suggested list for the basic contents of a first aid kit, which includes:

- ✔ a basics of first aid guide
- ✔ plasters
- ✔ eye pads
- ✔ triangular bandages
- ✔ safety pins
- ✔ wound dressings
- ✔ disposable gloves.

Activity

Think about the different areas of the school and the activities that take place in each subject area. Create a list of the first aid equipment that should be made available in each of the subject areas.

Appointed first aid personnel

The minimum requirement in a low-risk work environment is for one member of staff to be appointed to take responsibility for first aid in the workplace – this would include stocking and replenishing first aid kits and informing staff of what to do if they are injured. The individual does not have to be trained in how to administer first aid. In larger organisations or high-risk workplaces, the HSE makes the following recommendations for first aid personnel on site:

Low risk	Fewer than 25 staff	At least one person appointed to take charge of first aid provision
	25–50 staff	At least one trained first aider
	More than 50 staff	At least one trained first aider for every 100 members of staff employed
High risk	Fewer than 5 staff	At least one person appointed to take charge of first aid provision
	5–50 staff	At least one trained first aider
	More than 50 staff	At least one trained first aider for every 100 members of staff employed

There are a number of different first aid courses, covering different types of injury, that employees can be sent on. It is the responsibility of the employer to find the most appropriate course to ensure that staff are competent to deal with injuries.

Fire Safety Regulations

In Scotland, businesses are required to comply with the **Fire (Scotland) Act 2005** and the **Fire Safety (Scotland) Regulations 2006**. As with the legislation for first aid in the workplace, fire safety regulations also base the appropriate precautions on the type of work carried out in the workplace and a risk assessment of the workplace. The risk assessment determines what risks are in the building and how these can be reduced. It also helps to determine the type of fire alert and suppression systems that may be needed – taking into account the size of building and type of work that is being undertaken. The table below shows the areas that businesses should consider under the regulations.

Area	What employers must consider
Fire safety policy	All business must have a fire safety policy which includes arrangements for planning, organisation, control, monitoring and review of fire safety measures. Additionally, there must be one named person within each premises who has responsibility for co-ordinating fire safety measures.
Emergency fire action plan	The plan is the responsibility of management and should detail the actions that staff should take in the event of a fire.
Training	Staff should be made familiar with the policy and procedures that are in place for dealing with fire – this also includes how their actions can help to reduce the risk of fire, how to maintain fire equipment and what to do if there is a fire. This should happen at regular intervals and not just be a one-off event. Some staff may be identified as having specific duties in the event of a fire. These fire marshals should receive specific and regular training.
Drills	Regulations suggest that drills should be held at least once a year, but the frequency will depend on the type of premises and risks identified in the risk assessment. For example, it is recommended that schools hold a drill once a term. The drill gives staff the opportunity to put into practice the fire action plan. Regulations suggest that scenarios are enacted to simulate a real fire evacuation, such as blocking the use of escape routes so staff have to find an alternative method of escape. It may be useful to have some staff observe the fire drill to identify any issues so that procedures can be adapted.
Maintenance	Fire safety equipment has specifications for how frequently checks should be made. This can range from daily checks to ensure exits are not blocked, to weekly checks that the fire alarm system is working, to annual service checks on fire extinguishers.
Record keeping	Larger organisations have to maintain records on issues identified in the risk assessment and action taken, along with the results of maintenance and testing. These may be audited by authorities to ensure that the regulations are being met.
Prevention of fire	Housekeeping and storage – keeping potentially combustible material stored in appropriate places is essential. This can also include ensuring that waste is regularly removed and stored in a larger, covered bin until collection. Cleaning materials should be stored in a locked cupboard after use. Furniture – consideration will need to be given to the type of furniture that is purchased, depending on the type of work being undertaken by the organisation. Furniture needs to meet minimum safety standards and be maintained to ensure any rips or tears don't allow internal filling to be exposed. Electrical – electrical faults are often a major cause of fires. Staff should be trained to use equipment correctly to reduce the risk of faults. Equipment should be regularly tested and any faults reported should be repaired swiftly. Staff should be discouraged from trying to fix faults if they are not trained to do this.

Workplace (Health, Safety and Welfare) Regulations 1992

This legislation sets down the minimum accommodation standards that are required of nearly all types of workplaces in the UK. Providing staff with a comfortable working environment is essential to ensure that staff work effectively, and many organisations go above and beyond the minimum requirements to ensure that staff welfare is of a high standard. Some of the requirements of the regulations are given below:

Requirement	Details
Ventilation	Fresh, clean air should be circulated throughout the workplace. Ventilation should also reduce or remove warm, humid air. This can be achieved simply by having windows, but it may be necessary to provide a mechanical system, which should be regularly maintained.
Temperatures	Finding a temperature that suits everyone is difficult to achieve; however, the minimum requirement is for the workplace to be at least 16°C in most workplaces. There is no legal maximum temperature, but there is a requirement for the building to be at a comfortable level and employers may have to consider measures to ensure that this is achieved – through fans or portable air conditioning units.
Lighting	Lighting should be sufficient to allow staff to work and move around safely. Automatic emergency lighting must be provided where loss of light through a power cut or emergency would create a risk.
Room dimensions and space	There should be sufficient space for staff to work and move around the building. At least 11 cubic metres of space should be provided for each employee – though this may not be enough depending on the work being undertaken.
Toilets and washing facilities	Sufficient facilities should be provided for the number of staff in the organisation. These should be clean, well-lit and ventilated, and provide hot and cold running water, soap and clean towels or other methods of drying. Showers may also be provided depending on the type of work being undertaken by staff.
Facilities to rest and eat meals	A supply of high-quality drinking water should be provided for staff either from a mains supply or bought in in containers. Suitable seating should be provided for staff to take a rest from their normal work. There should be equipment provided for staff to store, prepare and heat their own food – especially where there is no vendor nearby that will provide this.

Health and Safety (Display Screen Equipment) Regulations 1992

(with some small changes being made by the Health and Safety [Miscellaneous Amendments] Regulations 2002)

Display Screen Equipment (DSE) are devices or equipment that have an alphanumeric or graphic display screen and include display screens, monitors, laptops, touch screens and other similar devices.

DSE can give rise to a variety of ill health conditions when used habitually. The most prevalent damage to users is repetitive strain injury (RSI), which is a general term used to describe the pain felt in muscles, nerves and tendons caused by repetitive movement and overuse. These regulations only apply to employers whose employees regularly use DSE for a significant part of their normal work (daily, for continuous periods of an hour or more).

According to the NHS, back pain is responsible for 7.6 million lost work days every year – a major cause of back pain is poor posture.

Some employees may experience fatigue, eye strain, upper limb problems and backache from over or improper use of DSE. These problems can also be experienced from poorly designed workstations or work environments. The causes may not always be obvious and can be due to a combination of factors.

Employers therefore must:

✓ consult with all employees using DSE

✓ analyse workstations to assess and reduce risks, seating, desk height, *etc.*

✓ provide safety equipment – such as anti-glare screens, wrist rests

✓ provide information and training – to prevent injury such as RSI and back pain

✓ provide eye and eyesight tests on request, and special spectacles, if needed

✓ encourage regular breaks to avoid stress-related problems or muscular problems

✓ review the assessment when the DSE changes (or the employee changes workstation).

Activity

- Search for information on Display Screen Equipment Regulations. Click on the link to Regulations and guidance equipment.
- Download and save and/or print the pdf file – 'Working with display screen equipment (DSE)–A brief guide'. *If printing – use multiple style – two per page.*
- Next download and save and/or print the pdf file – 'Workstation checklist' – complete this list for your own workstation.
- Prepare a training presentation outlining the basic requirements of the employer for DSE. Your presentation should contain **no more than six slides**. Save the presentation with a suitable filename – you may be asked to present this to your group.

Exam-style questions practice

11 Outline **three** strategies an Administrative Assistant could use to comply with the requirements of the Health and Safety Act. (3 marks)

12 Describe **two** key responsibilities employers have with regards to Display Screen Equipment regulations. (4 marks)

13 Compare the health and safety responsibilities of employers and employees in the workplace. (2 marks)

Workplace regulations – data handling

General Data Protection Regulations (GDPR) 2018

In May 2018 new regulations were brought in to comply with stricter rules on data processing from the EU. This regulation is relevant to all businesses, large or small, which process information on individuals. The type of personal data held may include name, phone number and address or financial details, medical and criminal records and employment history, and can take the form of paper or computer records. Due to the complexity of data handling legislation, GDPR recommends some types of organisation appoint a Data Protection Officer to oversee the organisation's policies and procedures to ensure compliance.

Personal data can be defined as information about living, identifiable individuals. The data does not need to be particularly sensitive information – it could just be a person's name and address. Sensitive information covers areas such as a person's racial or ethnic origin, political opinions or religious beliefs. Sensitive information can only be processed in certain restricted circumstances such as when the individual involved has freely given explicit written consent to its use for clearly stated purposes, the data is required for legal reasons or the information is needed for ethnic or anti-discriminatory monitoring.

If a business is subject to the Regulation, there are several legal responsibilities:

- All organisations must **register** with the **Information Commissioner** and pay a fee. The Commissioner must be notified about the processing and holding of personal data, the type of information a business processes and the purposes for which it is used. This information is placed on a public register called the Register of Controllers.
- Any personal data held by a company must be processed according to the **seven General Data Protection Regulation Principles** that state the requirements that have to be complied with under the 2018 legislation:

Principle	Requirements to comply
1 Lawfulness, fairness and transparency	Data must only be collected if there are valid reasons for doing so. Using the data must not breach any other laws and must not be used in a way that is detrimental or misleading to the individual.
2 Purpose limitation	From the outset, you must make it clear to the individual the purpose for using their data. A record of the purpose must be recorded with the Information Commissioner's Office (ICO) and a statement given to the individual (privacy statement). If the organisation decides it wants to do something different with the data, it must obtain consent.
3 Data minimisation	There are three areas for organisations to consider under this principle: ● **Adequate** – they must ensure that there is the right amount of data to achieve the purpose stated. ● **Relevant** – there must be a clear link between the purpose and the data collected. ● **Limited to what is necessary** – there must not be extra data that is not needed and will not be used for the purpose stated.
4 Accuracy	Organisations are responsible for ensuring that the data they have collected remains up to date, if necessary. They must demonstrate that they have taken reasonable steps to ensure the accuracy of the data or have considered erasing the data.

5	Storage limitation	Organisations must not keep data longer than necessary – it will be up to individual organisations to decide what length of time data should be kept before it is destroyed. This is called a retention policy. Organisations need to justify the time frame they have specified on their retention policy. Regular reviews should take place on the data held to consider whether the data should be erased or anonymised if it is no longer needed or being used.
6	Integrity and confidentiality	This principle is considered the security principle. Organisations must ensure that they have appropriate security measures in place to protect the data that is held.
7	Accountability	Organisations must take responsibility for the data that they hold and what happens to it. They must have relevant documentation in place to demonstrate their compliance with this regulation.

- **Consent** – there is a high expectation from the regulations that the individual has choice and control over their data and its use. The methods used to obtain consent must be clear and concise – there must be a statement, and this should be kept separate from any other terms and conditions to avoid confusion. Consent must be opt-in – organisations cannot pre-tick boxes, for example – and the individual must give explicit consent. Organisations must then retain the consent documentation for future reference.
- **Individual rights** – GDPR specifies **eight** rights that the individual has over their data and its use:
    1. The right to be informed
    2. The right of access
    3. The right to rectification
    4. The right to erasure
    5. The right to restrict processing
    6. The right to data portability
    7. The right to object
    8. Rights in relation to automated decision making and profiling

Note

See https://ico.org.uk/ for-organisations/guide-to-the-general-data-protection-regulation-gdpr/individual-rights/ for further information on these rights and how organisations have to implement them.

- **Data Protection Impact Assessments** (DPIA) – where an organisation is processing highly sensitive data then a DPIA must be completed. The DPIA must:
    - describe how and why the data is being processed
    - assess the need to collect the data and the measures that are going to be put in place to comply with the regulations
    - identify and assess risks to individuals
    - identify any additional measures to reduce or remove the identified risks.

    If, after completing the DPIA, it is found that the risks cannot be significantly reduced then the ICO can provide advice and support – they may also issue a warning not to process the data or ban it completely if they feel the risk is too great.
- **Data breaches** – a breach is when data is lost or stolen or may be when data has been accidentally sent to the wrong person. Where a data breach occurs, the organisation must report this to the ICO within 72 hours of becoming aware of the breach. If the data breach contains personal and sensitive data, then the organisation must notify the individuals affected as soon as possible. Failure to comply with this requirement will result in large fines – anything from €2 million or 2 per cent of global turnover.

- **International transfer** – GDPR sets out that data must only be transferred within the European Union. This is because all member states must comply with the regulations and so individual data can be protected, which cannot be guaranteed in countries outside the EU. There are exemptions to this rule and organisations must liaise with the ICO to determine what measures are needed to be in place to share data. One of the main requirements is that the individual must have given explicit consent for this to happen, but other conditions will also be stipulated.

Note

The UK also has its own data handling legislation – Data Protection Act (DPA) 2018. GDPR gives countries scope to set down how they will enforce the legislation and the organisations that will be involved in this; for example, the UK has the Information Commissioner's Office (ICO). Both GDPR and DPA must be used together when organisations are working with personal data.

Activity

- Prepare a presentation detailing the measures that businesses must implement to comply with the seven principles of the regulations. The presentation should be no more than eight slides long and should incorporate graphics.

OR
- Prepare a short report – written or word processed and no more than 200 words long – detailing the rules.

Freedom of Information Act 2000

Freedom of Information Act 2000 provides access to information held by public authorities. This means that public authorities are obliged to publish certain information about their activities; and, members of the public are entitled to request information from public authorities.

The Act covers any recorded information that is held by a public authority in England, Wales and Northern Ireland, and by UK-wide public authorities based in Scotland. *Information held by Scottish public authorities is covered by Scotland's own* **Freedom of Information (Scotland) Act 2002**.

The Act does not give people access to their own personal data such as their health records or credit reference file – this is already covered by the Data Protection Act. The main principle behind freedom of information legislation is that people have a right to know about the activities of public authorities, unless there is a good reason for them not to.

Note

ico is the UK's independent authority set up to uphold information rights in the public interest – https://ico.org.uk

Briefly, the Freedom of Information legislation states that:
- everyone has a right to access official information
- a requester of information does not need to give a reason for wanting the information
- all requests for information must be treated equally – regardless of who they are from
- only information that can be released to the world at large qualifies for disclosure.

Computer Misuse Act 1990

This is an Act to make provision for securing computer material against unauthorised access or modification; and for connected purposes:
- Accessing computer material without permission, for example, looking at someone else's files.
- Accessing computer material without permission with intent to commit further criminal offences, for example, hacking into the bank's computer and wanting to increase the amount in your account.
- Altering computer data without permission, for example, writing a virus to destroy someone else's data, or actually changing the money in an account.

At present, there are ongoing discussions about amending the law to define smartphones (i.e. those with internet browsers and other connectivity features) as computers under the Act. This amendment may also introduce a new offence of *making information available with intent*, i.e. publicly disclosing a password for someone's phone or computer so that others can access it illegally.

Activity

Search the internet for hints on how to create a secure password. Create a poster to inform staff of how to do this.

Copyright, Designs and Patents Act 1988

When you buy software (for example), copyright law forbids you from:
- giving a copy to an other person
- making a copy and then selling it
- using the software on a network (unless licenced)
- renting the software without the permission of the copyright holder.

Exam-style questions practice

14 Describe the rights of the individual as outlined in the General Data Protection Regulations. (4 marks)

15 Outline **four** methods of good information handling that should be employed by an organisation. (4 marks)

16 Explain **two** strategies that could be used to comply with effective data protection handling. (2 marks)

17 Discuss how effective data management can be ensured within an organisation. (6 marks)

5 Managing information and maintaining security and confidentiality

Managing information

With so much information available to us, it becomes even more important to make sure we take the time to ensure this information is managed correctly.

Most information is now stored electronically, although paper-based records still exist in many organisations. We are going to focus on electronic information; however, many of the points raised are still relevant to a paper-based system.

Take a look at your own My Documents – I'm sure it is very organised!

This is an example of a poorly organised file directory:

There are lots of different files types, names and versions. It will be difficult to easily navigate your way through all of this.

All organisations will operate a similar system to that operated in your school/college. Files will be named and saved in folders in different parts of the network. In a shared area of the network it is important that someone oversees the structure of the area where files are saved otherwise it would become a mess and impossible to find anything. This role is often referred to as Information Architect – someone who plans the way that files will be stored in a network. Organisations will set out some rules on how files are to be stored.

Naming conventions – These are rules on what files should be called. This will help ensure files can be found quickly and easily. Here's an example of a naming convention for a file:

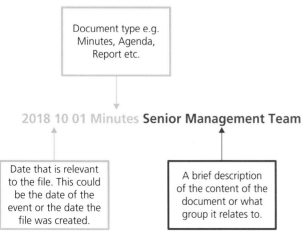

Document type e.g. Minutes, Agenda, Report etc.

2018 10 01 Minutes **Senior Management Team**

Date that is relevant to the file. This could be the date of the event or the date the file was created.

A brief description of the content of the document or what group it relates to.

It may seem over the top to have these types of rules for file naming, but when you are dealing with thousands of files it is important that you can find what you need quickly – imagine if everyone just called a file 'Report' or even worse 'Doc1, Doc2' – it would be impossible to find anything and waste so much time.

Having files saved in this way will also make it easier to search for files – rather than searching for the file, users can type in key words from the file name and the system will return documents that match the criteria. If files are named in a specific way, then it will make searches for files easier – if you are looking for minutes of a meeting that took place on a certain date, then if you use the convention above, you would be able to find the file you need very quickly.

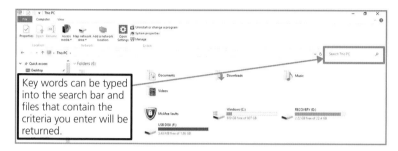

Key words can be typed into the search bar and files that contain the criteria you enter will be returned.

Folders also need to be created so that files can be grouped together, reducing the time taken to scroll through lists of files.

Once the files are in the network and stored correctly, there needs to be maintenance to make sure these files are up to date. If they are no longer needed they should be archived or deleted. It is useful for documents to have a specific owner, i.e. someone who takes responsibility for the file. Files should be checked on an annual basis to make sure they are still relevant and needed. Organisations will have a retention policy in place; this will state that a file should be archived for a certain period and then permanently deleted after this time has passed.

When dealing with people's personal information[1], it is important that an annual check is made on this data. You have probably seen this happen in school, where your contact details are sent home to be checked, for example, telephone numbers, address, medical details – this allows the schools to have the most up-to-date information. Most organisations will conduct this exercise with their staff and will remind their customers to update them if their details change.

Benefits of good file management

✓ **Makes it easier and faster to find the information staff need** – improves productivity and staff are not wasting time trying to find files.

✓ **Reduces the chances of information being lost** – which can be a big issue if someone's personal information is lost as this would be a breach of data protection.

(1) See page 18 for information on General Data Protection Regulations

✓ **Having a central system means all staff are accessing the same information** and reduces the chances of someone using out-of-date information.

✓ **Saves space on the network**, because there are no duplicates made of files and files that are no longer needed are removed.

Exam-style questions practice

18 Describe the steps that can be taken to make sure that information is managed effectively on a computer network. (3 marks)
19 Explain the consequences of failing to manage information on a computer network. (4 marks)
20 Justify the time taken to manage electronic information. (3 marks)

Keeping information secure and confidential

Information is vital to an organisation's success, they need it to make decisions and be able to contact people. This information is often private and contains sensitive information, for example, the personal details of their customers and staff. There is also information that may not seem confidential at first, but in the hands of a competitor could mean a business has lost its edge, for example, sales data, details of new products or advertising campaigns.

Here are the steps that organisations can take to keep information secure and confidential, when it is stored electronically:

Method	Description
Passwords	Computers should require a password to access them. Staff should be given their own username and password – this will allow different access rights to be issued. Passwords should be changed regularly to reduce the risk of them being cracked. Strong passwords have a mixture of letters (both upper and lower case), numbers and symbols. As an added level of security, it is also possible to add passwords to files, so that if a file is placed in the wrong location, it still cannot be read by everyone.
Access levels	In a networked system it is possible to give different members of staff different access to different folders, programs and places in the network. This means staff only have access to the information they need to complete their job. This reduces the risk of breaches to data protection legislation. For example, not all staff need to see the contact details of members of staff – this is likely to be something only a manager needs and the staff in the Human Resources Department.
Encryption	Encrypting a file or device is an added layer or security that means that if files or devices are taken, they cannot be read without the correct passphrase being entered to decrypt the file. When highly sensitive information has to be transmitted by email or on an external storage device, it is often a requirement from a company policy that files are encrypted to prevent the files being accessed if the data is lost or stolen.

Method	Description
Firewalls	A firewall is a piece of software that is installed to reduce the risk of hacking – which can allow your files to be stolen or corrupted by an external source. Firewall software needs to be kept up to date as hackers are always finding new ways to bypass security systems – you will have seen news articles of where hackers have stolen data from well-known organisations.
Anti-virus software	Anti-virus software prevents dangerous programs being installed on to your computer system which will corrupt and destroy files, so that they cannot be used again. Computer viruses spread easily on a network where everything is connected and so having an anti-virus software installed will help prevent this. As with firewalls, anti-virus software has to be updated regularly to detect new viruses that are developed.
Company policies	Organisations will have policies in place to guide staff on how to maintain security and confidentiality of information. This can be as simple as remembering to log off and lock screens when you are not at your computer. It can also go as far as banning the use of external storage devices, such as pen drives, so that information is not removed from the network, which increases the chance of it being lost and getting into the wrong hands. With staff now making use of mobile devices – there will be a requirement to have a password on these and to enable tracking software, so that if a mobile or tablet is lost it can be located or instructions sent to it to wipe the data from it to prevent unauthorised access to information. There will also be steps on what to do when taking devices out of the workplace, for example, not leaving your laptop in your car or unattended if you are travelling on public transport.

There are lots of things to consider when planning how to protect your information but it is essential to keep on top of them and continue to review practices as criminal organisations are always coming up with new ways to steal data.

Activity

- Access a news website and search for stories of where companies have been in the news for losing personal information of their staff or customers.
- Keep a copy of the article in your file.
- Highlight any points from the article – how it happened, what did the company do wrong or could have done better, what is it doing to support the people affected?

Some of the consequences of failing to give data security the importance it deserves are:

✗ **Data will be stolen** – this can lead to some embarrassing conversations with staff and customers, whose personal data might now be in the hands of a criminal organisation.

✗ **The organisation will receive bad publicity**, as news organisations often pick up on the latest data breaches. This will damage the company's reputation and it may lose customers as a result and struggle to gain new customers.

✗ **The data the company holds may be destroyed and corrupted** and if a backup has not been created recently and stored separately to the main network – this information may be irretrievable.

✗ **The company's network may need to be rebuilt** to destroy the virus that has caused the problem. There is a financial cost here of having to bring in a specialist to sort the problem, but also will mean the network will not be accessible to staff, so they cannot do their job fully until the network is restored – causing a loss of productivity.

✗ **The company will suffer financially** – if staff or customers' personal information is stolen and this is used, meaning they suffer a financial loss (for example, if bank details are stolen and money is removed from the bank account), the company will have to pay to replace this and cover any costs involved in preventing this happening again.

✗ If confidential information is stolen, the Information Commissioner is likely to become involved in investigating what went wrong – ultimately if the organisation is found not to have done done enough to prevent this happening in the first place, it will receive a fine.

Exam-style questions practice

21 Describe procedures organisations may put in place to help reduce the risk of information being lost or stolen. (4 marks)

22 Describe the steps that should be taken when taking confidential information out of the office on a portable device. (3 marks)

23 Explain the consequences of failing to have adequate procedures in place to protect information held on a network. (6 marks)

6 Impact of IT on the workplace

Every year new technology is integrated in many different workplaces with the aim of improving the working conditions of employees and business managers. Technology makes it possible to *telecommute*, work from *virtual* offices and *communicate* with businesses and individuals across the world. Employees no longer have to be restricted to one workplace as new technology enables employees to work from anywhere.

Also, video conferencing tools have simplified the way we hold meetings at work, reducing and sometimes completely stopping the need to travel for business meetings – saving both time and money.

Contracts/working practices

Traditionally, most working practices were office based and consisted simply of full-time, part-time, job share and flexi-time. However, much more flexible working practices are becoming extremely popular because so many duties and responsibilities can be accomplished while the employee is travelling or from an employee's home.

With the help of modern technology, home-working, hot-desking and video conferencing have become common practice, meaning that the conventional business environment is evolving. Organisations that have embraced changes in working practices are finding that not only are they cutting costs but also that staff morale among their workforce is increasing.

The benefits of flexible working practices facilitated by the increase in the use of IT in the workplace can be summarised as follows.

Benefits to the organisation may include:	Benefits to the employee may include:
● an ability to retain trained and valuable staff – when their personal circumstances change	● an ability to continue to work when personal circumstances change
● increase in productivity due to increased staff morale	● an ability to achieve a good work–life balance
● decrease in staff absence due to flexibility of work practices	● reduced stress levels
● staff may be more motivated as they recognise the organisation is tailoring the job to suit their needs.	● greater level of job satisfaction and be able to maintain a proper career path/personal development.

Why is work–life balance important?

Work–life balance is dynamic. Life changes constantly and an individual's needs change too. Work–life balance is achieved when an individual's right to a life inside and outside paid work is accepted and respected to the mutual benefit of the organisation and the individual. *Achieving a good work–life balance is the responsibility of both the organisation and the individual.* When an organisation promotes flexible working and makes the best use of new technologies, it can access a much wider pool of possible employees.

Impact of IT on workflow

Employees no longer have to be tied to one workplace; new mobile technology tools like tablets, smartphones and laptops enable employees to work from anywhere. This leads to great flexibility in working enabling, for example, home-working, or working while travelling and tele-working. Increasingly, networking 'hot spots' are being provided in public areas that allow connection back to the office network or the internet. The growth of cloud computing has also impacted positively on the use of mobile devices, supporting more flexible working practices by providing services over the internet.

Most organisations have their own website to allow direct communication with other organisations, and current and potential customers. Within the organisation, however, the use of an intranet, email and web or video conferencing have completely changed the face of the modern workplace.

● **Intranet** – is a private network that is contained **within** an organisation. It normally consists of many interlinked local area networks (i.e. within the organisation only) and also has access to the wide area network (i.e. the world wide web). The main purpose of an intranet is to share the organisation's information and computing resources among employees. An intranet can also be used to facilitate working in groups and for teleconferences. Employees have easy access to files but there is no access to the general public. It also allows for easy shared access to equipment such as printers.

- **Email** – almost all employees have an email account. When email was first used, employees sent emails as part of their daily administrative work but did not really expect an immediate answer. Nowadays, because of the increased use of mobile technology, employees can check and respond to email on their mobile devices which has created a work culture where employees are expected to respond to emails right away – and sometimes many are expected to do so at the weekends too.
- **Video/web conferencing** – video conferencing tools have simplified the way work meetings are held, meaning that it is not always necessary to have to travel to a single location to meet with colleagues. This practice is extremely popular and saves both time and money.

In other words, IT has very positive impacts on the workplace which can be summarised as follows:

- **Communication within the workplace is simplified:** employees and managers can use different communication tools, for example:
  - **Skype®:** a software program which allows face-to-face communication using mobile devices – laptops, tablets, smartphones, etc.
  - **WhatsApp:** a cross-platform mobile messaging app which allows you to exchange messages. In addition, WhatsApp users can create groups, send each other unlimited images, video and audio messages.
- **Security of data within the workplace:** many organisations have resorted to cloud data hosting services like Dropbox, Amazon Cloud Drive, etc. to secure their business data. Employees with permission can access these data from anywhere using smartphones or tablets while still being secure as cloud hosting services ensure that all data saved on their servers are encrypted and all accounts are password protected.
- **Improvement in efficiency within the workplace:** new technology saves time because it automates most difficult tasks, e.g. accounting software can track an inventory, manage sales, manage customer contact and calculate tax returns, and so much more.

There are, of course, costs involved in setting up the equipment and training required to make use of mobile devices. Mobile IT devices can expose valuable data to unauthorised people if the proper precautions are not taken to ensure that the devices, and the data they can access, is kept safe.

Note

In a recent study, it was found that 38 per cent of employees routinely check work emails at the dinner table, 50 per cent do so while still in bed, and 69 per cent won't even go to bed without first checking their emails!

Office layout

More organisations have introduced an open-plan layout to facilitate the change in working practices. However, now that wireless technology has improved communication, sharing of files and resources, the need for open-plan is not quite as important as it once was. In fact, recent surveys suggest that open-plan is not as effective as previously thought and in fact can sometimes have a negative effect on productivity and morale.

Note

Most successful IT companies, like Google, Facebook, Apple Inc. and Microsoft, use new technology to improve working conditions and experience for their staff. Employees at Facebook have a dedicated section for playing video games, because they believe that games make people relax and they get prepared for new tasks at work.

Just imagine an employee working at a computer without having any social interaction breaks – they may get very bored and as a result their output would probably be low, or they can even lose interest in completing the job effectively. So, owners and managers can use technology to boost employee morale – letting them feel comfortable while at work.

Exam-style questions practice

24 Describe a benefit of flexi-time to:
  a) the organisation, and
  b) the employee. (4 marks)
25 Describe the benefits of home-working for an employee. (4 marks)
26 Discuss the factors regarding IT that need to be considered for employees who want to start working from home. (6 marks)

Chapter 2
Customer care in administration

What you should know

There are **two** topics to this chapter. By the end of this chapter you should be able to:

1 Understand the benefits of good, and consequences of poor, customer care.
2 Understand the mechanisms for monitoring and evaluating the quality of customer care.

1 Customer care

The customer is always right.

Why? In 2017, approximately £369 million was spent in retailers (figures from the Office for National Statistics). That's a huge amount of money and, of course, there are lots of businesses trying to get people to spend money with them rather than the competition. With fierce competition on the high streets and now of course online, often you can find the same product or service in many different stores and the prices are often fairly similar, so what makes customers choose one place over the other? Most would agree that it is often down to the level of service received.

Activity

- In groups, discuss experiences you have had as a customer.
- Make a note of the worst experience your group has faced and a note of the best experience you have had.
- Prepare a presentation to report the group's findings.

The UK has a poor reputation for customer service, with many hit TV programmes being about solving issues in this area. According to customers these are some of their biggest bug bears about customer service:

- Being passed around different members of staff.
- Staff talking to each other when serving a customer.
- Long queues or being on hold for long periods of time.
- Rude staff.
- Lack of knowledge.

Which? Survey www.mirror.co.uk/news/ampp3d/one-thing-annoys-customers-most--4269724

You will probably agree that you have seen this happen to you or someone you know. It's also not a very complicated issue, yet so many organisations still get it wrong. Let's look at what businesses should be trying to do or avoid doing.

What does good customer service look like?

Even in the most difficult of situations, when a customer is angry and frustrated about an issue that might not be the fault of the member of staff dealing with the customer, it is vital for the staff member to remain calm and listen to the customer. Providing excellent customer service in the first place, might avoid this. Here are some common practices that businesses use:

Customer care policy – organisations that truly have customer service at the core of their business will have a written policy detailing what promises and guarantees the organisation will make to their customers. It will help support staff in providing good customer care by detailing what should happen in different circumstances. This will help make sure that customers are all dealt with consistently and fairly, which is especially important when a business has multiple stores.

Staff training – good customer care is a skill that is learned and developed. During induction training, new staff must be shown what the business expects from its staff when customers are being served. It must not end there. Staff must have ongoing training to maintain the levels of service, no matter how long the member of staff has worked for the organisation. Some organisations may also go as far as to offer a qualification in customer care which can be obtained by completing on-the-job training. Often businesses will also have reminders and prompts to staff around the organisation; posters in staff areas, stickers or pop-ups on phones, computer displays or tills and cards with hints and tips for staff. Giving customer care this status shows to staff and customers that it is a very important aspect of the business.

What is a customer care policy?

A customer care policy is a document which states how a customer will be treated in different circumstances, particularly when a customer complains.

The document is often positive, giving steps on how to provide excellent customer service, to avoid a complaint in the first place. Detailed guidelines could include:

- what to say when answering the phone
- rules on the maximum length of time in which a complaint must be responded to
- how to deal with complaints
- what staff members can offer to customers to settle a complaint and what situations might warrant contacting a more senior member of staff

- advice for dealing with customers who are angry and may be confrontational over a complaint.

Depending on the type and size of the organisation, the policy may have very detailed guidance on every situation possible. The organisation must make sure that good training is provided so that staff can deal with any unexpected situations that may not be included – there are always new and unexpected circumstances and staff must be prepared to act on their feet.

Why should organisations care about customer service?

When organisations get customer service right, there are a number of benefits:

- ✓ **Repeat custom**: delivering excellent customer care will provide a lasting memory and customers will return to use the business again. Repeat business will mean repeat sales and this will help the business to have a healthy profit in the long term. Research also shows that it is cheaper to retain existing customers than to try to attract new customers. This is because to attract new customers there needs to be advertising and offers to entice customers to your business – this costs a lot of money. A lot of what good customer care is about actually costs nothing at all.
- ✓ **Reputation**: if customers have a good experience they will tell others. This is free advertising and there can't be anything better than being known for providing excellent customer care. More new customers, on top of keeping your existing customers, will further increase sales and therefore profit, securing the future of the business. This also means there are high expectations from customers and the pressure will be on to prove you are as good as everyone says.
- ✓ **Complaints are reduced**: if you provide excellent service, there is less chance that customers will want or need to complain. Dealing with complaints is a very challenging task for staff and dealing with negatives day in, day out will not necessarily provide a very enjoyable working environment. If businesses take service seriously and have it at the heart of the business, this will actively reduce complaints. This will also make sure staff work in a positive environment, where complaints have to be dealt with because there has been a serious failure and staff want to make things right. This will improve staff morale and reduce staff turnover rates.

On the other hand, where customer care is not given the correct status by business managers and leaders, which then results in this passing down to the staff on the shop floor, there can be serious consequences for businesses, including:

- ✗ **Loss of customers**: if a customer receives poor service they will likely go to a competitor instead. This can lead to other issues, as detailed below.

✗ **Damaged reputation**: if customers receive a poor service they are likely to tell others; in fact, it is more likely a customer will tell others about a bad experience than a good service. This will mean potential new customers will avoid using the business. With social media and review websites commonplace, a bad experience is now not only passed to customers' friends, it can be communicated nationally and globally very quickly. People will closely watch how businesses respond to customer complaints online.

✗ **Loss of sales**: as customers leave to go to competitors and new customers are put off from using the business, sales will fall as a result. This will mean less profit for the business and ultimately could mean the survival of the business is in doubt.

✗ **Poor staff morale**: where there isn't a focus on staff training to provide excellent customer care or even to provide the basic training to do their job, staff may become demotivated and demoralised. This, in itself, will mean a poor service will be provided. If on top of this customers begin to complain frequently, staff will become even more demotivated and not enjoy working for the organisation – they may choose to leave eventually. Word may spread of the organisation being a bad place to work and it may struggle to recruit new staff.

Exam-style questions practice

1 Describe the benefits of providing good customer service. (3 marks)
2 Explain the consequences of poor customer service. (5 marks)
3 Outline the features of an effective complaints procedure. (4 marks)

2 Monitoring customer care

When organisations have spent time and money investing in customer service, they will want to make sure that this has been well spent. There are a number of well-established practices, as well as some new and emerging modern practices, to check that customer care is up to standard and, if not, allows customers to provide feedback so the organisation can improve.

Customers will be asked to complete a questionnaire/survey about the service they have received. Customers will be asked to rate different aspects of the service they have received on a scale of good through to bad and then provide more detailed comments.

The surveys can take different forms:
● face-to-face discussion with a staff member where the survey is completed together
● on paper that they take away and return at a later date (often by post)
● over the telephone where they will be asked the questions
● online through an email link after they have purchased something.

The more traditional methods of surveys, such as postal, are used less and less, and businesses are using online surveys more frequently or asking

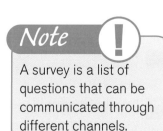

Note

A survey is a list of questions that can be communicated through different channels.

customers to complete an automated survey after a telephone call rather than speak to a person – this saves a significant amount of money but can increase the volume of responses received.

Survey type	Advantages	Disadvantages
Face-to-face	✓ A staff member can ask for further details from the customers, if they don't fully understand the feedback given. ✓ Easier to guarantee feedback is given from customers then and there, compared to other methods where response rates are lower.	✗ Customers may not give an accurate picture of their experience in front of a member of staff to avoid embarrassment, especially if the service was poor. ✗ Customers don't often like to be stopped, they may be busy and rush through the survey to get away.
Postal	✓ A large number of customers can be surveyed. ✓ Customers can take their time to complete the survey and may be more likely to give honest feedback.	✗ Response rate is low. ✗ Can be expensive to post the surveys out to customers and often a prize has to be offered to encourage returns.
Telephone	✓ Detailed responses can be given – either because a person is there to prompt a response or an automated system allows for a recording of comments to be left. ✓ A large number of customers can be surveyed quickly; this is certainly the case if customers are asked to complete a survey after the end of a call.	✗ Customers don't often like to be disturbed at home with a call, this is why many call centres now ask customers if they would be happy to complete a telephone survey after they have finished the call.
Online	✓ One of the cheapest methods of surveying customers. ✓ Responses are automatically collated and analysed – saving a member of staff having to input the data. Instant access is also provided to responses as soon as submitted.	✗ Can be a low response rate, especially as now so many businesses send these out when a purchase is made.

Social media

Most organisations now have a presence on social media. This has opened a two-way dialogue between the business and its customers that hasn't been possible before.

Customers use Twitter, Facebook, Instagram and many other sites to contact businesses for many reasons, but one which has to be managed very carefully by the organisation is when a customer makes a comment, especially if it is a negative comment – because everyone is watching the response!

Customers open the discussion first with a comment about the service they have received, they may make a comment or post a photo. Large organisations often have a dedicated social media team to deal with customer enquiries and comments and to provide a response. Where more detailed discussion and dialogue is needed often the company will try to take this into a more private environment, either an email, private message or phone call.

If managed correctly, social media can help businesses improve by using the feedback provided by customers. Customers are more open and honest when using social media and this can give businesses a greater insight into the customer experience. There are many dangers though – if the messages are not dealt with appropriately this could provide a backlash against the company and a lot of negativity. Customers' expectation for instant responses can be difficult to meet when staff may not be available to respond 24/7.

Mystery shopping

Organisations often employ mystery shoppers or contract specialist companies (such as ABA Research) to act as a normal customer or client and report back on the service they have received. A number of mystery shops are completed in different locations by different shoppers in order to give an overview of how customer service is across the business.

Staff are not aware that this is taking place, as the mystery shopper will not be known to the team being evaluated – the hope being to give a true reflection of what a real customer is experiencing. The mystery shopper will complete a survey and return it for the organisation to take on board any feedback given – which can be positive and negative.

Review sites

Businesses are now embracing online review sites (such as TripAdvisor, Trustpilot or Reevoo) and in some cases, company websites now have this facility to provide a review straightaway so that other customers can see comments.

Customers will be asked to rate the service received on different areas on a sliding scale. They will then be able to provide a more detailed comment. The business itself will also be able to follow up with a comment if it is needed.

Making use of this facility shows that the company cares about the views of its customers and it is done in an open and transparent way, so that the company cannot hide from the issues. As always, if the business has put in the effort to provide excellent service, the reviews should be mainly positive.

Focus groups

Most large businesses recruit volunteers from their regular customer base to join a focus group. These groups will meet at intervals throughout the year to discuss the customer experience and this allows managers and customers to enter into discussion on issues, big or small, to improve.

This is another pro-active approach that a business can use to show that they really care about the customer service they provide. They must not ignore a problem which could lead to a major complaint. Doing so would leave customers angry and staff under pressure to deal with these complaints. Talking to customers can help to find out the smaller issues and put in place steps to improve service so a major complaint is not received.

Activity

Design a survey to evaluate the experience of your school canteen.
- Think carefully about what types of questions you will want to ask and how you will break up the questions – food, seating areas, etc.
- Consider the best way to collect this information – online, face-to-face, a focus group.
- Collate the responses and prepare a short report to detail your findings.

As you have seen, there are many different methods to monitor and evaluate the customer experience. It is important that managers make use of this information to improve customer service.

Exam-style questions practice

4 Describe **two** methods of gathering customer feedback. (4 marks)
5 Compare electronic methods of gathering customer feedback to more traditional face-to-face or paper-based systems. (2 marks)

Chapter 3

Effectively managing information

What you should know

There are **two** topics to this chapter. By the end of this chapter you should understand how to:

1 Select appropriate methods of communication to disseminate complex information and to take account of the needs of the audience.

2 Make adjustments to remove potential barriers to communication to ensure information is received and understood.

1 Methods of communicating to different audiences

Effective communication is vital to the success of any organisation – it must be timely, clear and appropriate. Poor communication is often the cause of things going wrong because staff don't know what to do, because they might not have received the information or they have it but don't understand it. Organisations must take the time to plan for communication, particularly in a large organisation, where information can easily get lost in the many layers of management and staff.

There are many different ways of disseminating information to people, but the choice of method will depend on the audience receiving the information and the type of information that is being communicated.

Audience – when planning to communicate information, the presenter or manager must consider who is receiving the information. The experience of the audience will be crucial, as an audience that has some knowledge or experience of a topic will be dealt with very differently to an audience that has very little or no knowledge at all.

Type of information – there are a number of different methods that can be used to communicate information to people. Some are used on their own, but often more than one method is used to complement each other and provide support to the person receiving the information. Information can be communicated written or verbally in a face-to-face situation – in both cases it is possible to use traditional methods and more modern methods that involve the use of technology.

Written

Written communication will be presented as a document for a person to take and read to themselves – this can either be in paper form or provided electronically. Popular choices of written communication are:

Leaflet

Leaflets are a good way of summarising information that people need to refer to frequently. Leaflets will contain text and graphics to make it easy to take in the information that is being presented. It is a fairly cheap and easy method to produce and can be printed and distributed to staff or placed on a network for all to access.

Care needs to be taken to plan the leaflet – too much information will put people off reading and so this should be a summary with lots of bulleted lists, pictures to highlight key messages and short sentences and paragraphs that get to the point quickly.

A leaflet should be used to back up information that people already have, for example, a shortened version of a policy that can be used as a Quick Reference Guide or an Essential Information Guide that new staff can use after their induction training.

Poster

This is a fairly cheap and easy way to communicate information to a large number of people. At first it may seem quite a straightforward task to complete – but there are many points to consider to make a poster successful.

Posters will be displayed on walls or noticeboards that people will walk past or go near frequently – to get people to stop or to get the message across to the target audience in the few seconds that they are walking past is key to a poster's success. A good poster:

- grabs the audience's attention
- uses key pieces of text only that can be seen easily
- makes use of appropriate graphics to highlight the key message
- is clear and easy to read.

Digital technology

Digital technology is used to communicate information to different audiences.

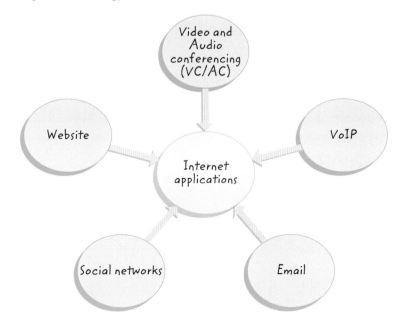

Email

Organisations will use emails as the main method of communication. It is a very useful tool for organisations for the following reasons:

- One message can be sent to **multiple** users at once.
- **Attachments** can be added – many different file types can be added (pictures, movie files, presentations, spreadsheets).
- If you want to make sure that the email has been opened, you can ask for a **read receipt**. This will send you a message back to say that your message was opened.
- Emails can be **accessed on mobile devices**, so even if people are out and about, they can still receive, read and respond to email messages.
- Messages and attachments can be **saved** for future reference.

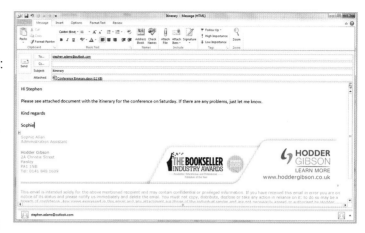

Emails are useful when a simple message needs to be passed on. In organisations most people use emails to pass on messages received. For example, someone called to speak to a member of staff while they were out for lunch and the message contains the details of the caller and their number to return a call, or after a meeting the minutes will be circulated around those that attended for them to check over and know what action points there are.

It can be easy just to email everything to everyone, but care needs to be taken so that the messages are not missed. Too many emails can lead to people glancing over messages and not reading them carefully, because they have so many to read in a day. Email messages should be passing on simple and straightforward messages or documents for people to read. Where a discussion starts to take place as a result of an email message or the content is very complex and needs further explanation, an email is possibly not the best choice of method and will need to be complemented with another method. For example, you might email round a new policy that is being implemented in the workplace for staff to read over and then a meeting or presentation will follow to explain how it will be implemented and take any questions. Simply emailing the document would lead to lots of issues in the long run.

E-diary

Electronic diaries are used to keep and share on computer networks. The use of e-diaries introduces flexibility to the format of diaries, presenting different views, such as by year, month or week. Unlike a paper diary, the computer automatically adds new pages when needed, extra room for each day, and retains copies of diaries for years gone past.

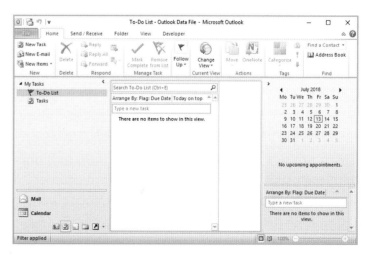

E-diaries are very useful as appointments can be scheduled easily – and repeated automatically if they are regular; for example, monthly, weekly or annually. If an appointment is changed or cancelled it can be easily amended or deleted, and a confirmation email can be sent to that effect. Access to e-diaries is normally internal and private to the organisation.

When setting up formal or informal meetings, the Senior Administrative Assistant can have access to everyone's diary and check for the most suitable date (for example, when everyone involved is free to attend and/or accommodation is available). When this is done, and all participants have been contacted via email, diaries can be updated automatically when the invitations have been accepted/declined. Alerts can also be set up to remind attendees a few days or hours before the meeting. This is also a useful tool for the Administrative Assistant to use – to chase up any requirements for the meeting being planned, such as room availability, IT equipment arranged, catering/special dietary requirements and disabled access.

As well as being part of the email system on a computer network, e-diaries also have the following useful features, which can help improve communication:

- personal calendaring
- automatic scheduling (for meetings, etc.)
- address book (contact lists)
- 'Post-it' style notes facility
- tasks list
- daily to-do lists.

Instant messaging

Organisations frequently make use of instant messaging (IM) such as WhatsApp or Google Hangouts™. This allows people to get in touch with staff when a quick question or discussion is needed, but where a meeting or phone call, which will interrupt the people's duties, is not necessary.

- IM systems allow one-to-one discussions or group chats.
- Users are able to set their status, so if they are busy, on the phone or away from the computer, people can leave a message so they are not disturbed.
- IM chat can be saved for future reference if needed.
- Some IM systems allow documents to be shared, in a similar way to emails.
- It is also possible to use the system for video chat, if suitable equipment is available on the computer or mobile device you are using.
- A message can be broadcast to all people signed into the IM system – this is useful if you need to send urgent messages that all users need to be aware of – for example, the network will be down in the evening for maintenance and users are to log off.

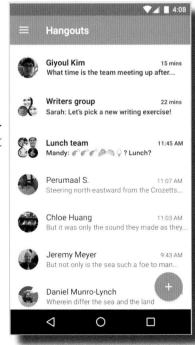

This is not just a method of communication that organisations use with their staff, they also use it with their customers. Many retail websites now offer the ability to chat online to a member of staff rather than place a call.

Network or Virtual Learning Environment

Most, if not all, organisations, will have a network of computers, allowing files to be shared.

Organisations will often have a central place that all staff can access and easily navigate where they can place policies, procedures and help guides for staff to refer to. Having documents in this central location means that everyone is able to access the same information. It also means that when an updated version is created, everyone has access to the most current version.

There is potential that staff may not go in and view this information regularly, or may print out a copy or save a copy to their My Documents, which could result in out-of-date information being used. It is possible to change file permissions to prevent documents being printed so out-of-date versions do not go into circulation.

It is often difficult to check that staff have actually read information and if they have you cannot be certain that they have understood it. As a solution to this many organisations have invested in Virtual Learning Environments (VLE), such as Moodle or SCHOLAR. These online environments look and feel very much like a website and can provide details of a policy or procedure that staff need to be aware of. To make the information more accessible to staff, as well as the usual text and graphics that would be seen in a leaflet or poster, video clips or sound bites can also be included to explain complex information.

Users are then required to complete a quiz, which will allow managers to see if the information has been understood and, where there are issues, can allow steps to be taken to address this. Some VLE systems will force staff to complete the training exercise in a certain period of time and it is possible to lock out access to the desktop until the training is completed successfully. This certainly overcomes the issues of staff not reading information that is stored in the network or just sent via an email.

Social media

Applications such as Facebook, Twitter, Google+ and YouTube are the latest additions to the growing methods of electronic communication available. In the UK, 58 per cent of adults have an account with a social network site that they access when at home. Organisations use these sites to post short pieces of information for interested people to view. Often people have to follow or like an organisation's page on a social network and so gives instant access to customers.

This method is a much more informal way of communicating. Messages have to be short and to the point, as there is a limit to how much text can added to each message. There is also no guarantee that everyone will see the message, if accounts are not checked regularly, as there are so many posts added to these networks, the message may get lost. Often organisations will post information on more than one social network, as well as on their website.

The information posted on these sites is open to the public – any posts or replies are visible to anyone – so organisations have to be careful about what they say and that no personal or confidential information is posted on the site.

Companies can use their social network sites to:
- Alert customers of problems or issues – for example, a store is closed, the website or phone line is down.
- Tell customers about offers or new products/services available.
- Post videos or photographs.
- Link to other websites with more detailed information.
- Ask customers questions for feedback.

Face-to-face

This method of communication is considered the most effective, as how better to pass on information than delivering it personally. It allows you to check that everyone has understood the message as you can see their body language (in most cases) and allows people to ask questions to clarify the message. It is also not easy to get right – you need to be able to keep the audience's attention and it can be difficult to deal with questions on the spot.

Presentation

Delivering a presentation often involves one person or a group of people speaking to a large audience. This method is good when a message needs to be passed on to a large group at once, for example, this might be the launch of a new product to staff or media (think of launches by major electronic firms such as Apple Inc., Microsoft or Sony Corporation).

Everyone receives the message at the same time, which is an advantage of this method of communication; however, it takes a very skilled presenter to make this method a success. The audience may still be able to ask questions, but in a large group some may not be confident enough to speak up if they are uncertain of any points.

What makes a good presentation:
- ✓ The presenter will have planned, practised and researched their presentation so they can deliver it confidently – which in turn will engage the audience.
- ✓ Presenter's style – the audience needs to be engaged and so the presenter needs to make good use of their voice and be animated and enthusiastic about the topic they are delivering, which will help keep the audience's attention.
- ✓ Appropriate use of presentation software – slides should be used to help guide the audience through the presentation and highlight key points. Often graphics are better to use than words. If the audience can get all the information they need from the slides, then there is no point in having a presentation in the first place. The audience is there to listen to the presenter.

✓ Equipment – with a large audience it is important that sound equipment is provided so that everyone is able to hear in all areas of the room. In large rooms a person's voice will fade as it travels – even the loudest of speakers will need to use a microphone. It might also be useful to film the presentation so that it can be used again. This would be important if not everyone could make the presentation but it is essential for everyone to hear the information.

The consequences of not following these simple steps are:

✗ People will become disengaged with the presentation and not pay attention if they find the presentation too boring – this may be because the topic is too complex for the target audience or the presenter is just reading from the slides on screen.

✗ If they become disengaged they might start talking to others in the audience – this distracts more people.

✗ Members of the audience might have started to talk to each other because they can't hear what is being said or they might not be able to see properly, if the screen has not been placed in good location.

Meetings

Meetings allow for people to gather together, usually in smaller groups, to share information and discuss. Meetings can be formal or informal.

A formal meeting will have a set of rules to follow and require specific documentation. This will mean that a record is kept, so that those attending and those who were not able to make the meeting are able to review what was said, discussed and agreed.

Documentation for formal meetings includes the following:

- A **Notice of Meeting** gives the date, time and place of the proposed meeting and an **Agenda** gives a list of items to be discussed.
  A well-constructed **agenda** should allow those attending to be able to:
  - prepare for the meeting by reading/researching any relevant paperwork before the meeting takes place (including facts and figures), allowing for more focused discussion during the meeting
  - decide whether their attendance is indeed necessary. In some instances, this could mean that instead of attending, they could make their contribution in writing or via another person.

    It also provides a controlled structure for the meeting and so avoids any random or off-point discussion – a timed structure assists with this. Some people may find the more formal setting intimidating and so choose not to speak, but a good chairperson will make sure that all members of the group are included and have the chance to speak.

- A **Chairperson's Agenda** is used in a formal meeting and is different from the normal agenda in that it has space on the right-hand side to allow the Chairperson to make notes **before** and **during** the meeting.
- **Minutes of a Meeting** are an organised record of those attending a meeting and the topics discussed. Minutes normally follow the

> **Hints & tips** ★
>
> *An agenda should be a short document – ideally a single page – with brief notes on items for discussion. This assures people that their attendance is important, and their contribution valued!*

same order as the agenda. They are **not** a word-for-word account of everything said but should give details of all proposals and outline any discussions and any decisions made.

- **Action Minutes** are similar to normal minutes except there is a separate column on the right-hand side outlining who is responsible for implementing a decision or course of action – **and** they usually include a timescale or deadline.

Duties of the Chairperson

The Chairperson should ensure that formal and informal meetings function properly, that there is full participation during meetings, that all relevant matters are discussed and that effective decisions are made and carried out.

Duties include:

- starting the meeting **on time** to ensure it does not overrun (not waiting for latecomers)
- ensuring the meeting has a **quorum** (the minimum number of people who need to attend a meeting according to the constitution) – otherwise the meeting will have to be postponed
- **approving** the minutes of the previous meeting (with the agreement of the other members of the meeting) as a true record
- dealing with any **matters arising** from the minutes of the previous meeting
- maintaining **good order** by ensuring participants are courteous, polite and non-aggressive
- allowing **adequate discussion** time for each item – while making sure that discussion is focused
- ensuring that everyone at the meeting has the opportunity to talk and **contribute** to any discussion
- **summing up discussions** prior to voting – highlighting important points and clarifying misunderstandings
- deciding when there has been adequate discussion and **calling a vote** – ensuring constitution rules are complied with
- make a **casting vote** if votes are tied
- bringing the meeting to a **close** – sometimes it is useful to ask for a brief evaluation of the meeting from the group
- **thanking** the group for their contributions and setting the **date and time** for the next meeting if appropriate – and asking the group for suggestions for the agenda.

> **Hints & tips**
>
> *Some groups schedule 15 minutes of time to socialise before the start of the meeting.*

Duties of the Administrative Assistant

The Administrative Assistant is usually the person who makes the arrangements for meetings, including AGMs, and keeps formal records of the group's process and decisions (the minutes of the meeting). The duties include the following:

Before the meeting

- Preparing the notice of meeting and agenda (in agreement with the Chairperson) – *making sure they are delivered to participants in good time*
- Finding/arranging the venue – *ensuring it is suitable for the purpose and size of the meeting*
- Arranging for any AV equipment required – *testing equipment to make sure it is in working order*
- Sending relevant documentation required for the meeting – *including minutes of the previous meeting – to allow those attending to prepare for any discussion*
- Ordering refreshments for attendees – *ensuring any dietary requirements are passed on to caterers*

During the meeting

- Making sure those attending sign the attendance register
- Issuing name badges – *if appropriate, for example when there are a large number of attendees*
- Taking the minutes – *make notes to ensure all discussion is properly recorded, and action points and decisions noted are accurate*

After the meeting

- Writing the draft minutes of the meeting – *for approval by the Chairperson*
- Making a note of the date and time of the next meeting in the diary – *an alert can be set to ensure the preparation for this is carried out in good time.*

Note

An informal meeting does not have any of the rules and requirements of the formal meeting and often just happens as and when needed; for example, on return from holiday, a manager may have a brief meeting to talk about what has happened while they were away.

Video/Audio Conference/Call

With the developments in mobile technology, as well as more traditional laptops and desktops, people from all over the world are now able to meet without the need to travel.

Although specialist Video and Audio Conferencing (VC/AC) systems exist, it is now possible to complete these with equipment that most people will have: laptop/desktop/mobile device. In order to allow the video call to take place you will require access to a webcam, along with a headset to hear and speak. With most modern tablets, smartphones and laptops, these features come as standard.

Video meetings take place when individuals communicate online regardless of their location. They can see and hear each other in real time.

Such meetings allow individuals to share data and information in real time without having to be present in a single physical location. This avoids the expense of travelling to a central location and improves efficiency as staff do not need to waste time travelling to the venue but can just join the meeting from their desk or from wherever they are based, if they are using mobile technology.

In addition to saving time and money, these online meetings are also more environmental friendly due to the reduction in the carbon footprint resulting from less travelling to and from meetings. These meetings (also referred to as **remote meetings**) are an excellent option for when distances between participants are significant.

Software from Microsoft® Lync™ or Adobe® Connect™ allows video calls from desktops, laptops or mobile devices but also allows for collaboration by letting users share what is on their screen. This allows users to discuss and make changes to documents. Some technical difficulties do still exist with this method of communication. When using a fixed internet connection in an office, at home or at a **wifi** hotspot, connections are often maintained; however, if relying on your mobile signal this can cause the connection to be lost. There is also the possibility of the charge running out on mobile devices as using this feature can cause a greater drain on the battery.

There are advantages to both meetings that take place in person and remote meetings as outlined in the table below:

Advantages of online meetings	Advantages of face-to-face meetings
They are usually relatively cheap to run.	Body language is easier to read face to face and therefore participants are more likely to pick up on a person saying something that conflicts with what they might be thinking.
Productivity is increased by saving on travel time to the meeting, if people are not in the same location.	They are better for giving sensitive feedback or bad news to individuals on a one-to-one basis.
Immediate decisions can be made across vast geographical distances.	There is a better chance of getting attendees' full attention as it is harder for people to multitask, for example, work on their computer while attending the meeting.

As you can see there is a huge range of different methods of communication available and the key to their success is choosing the one that is most suitable to the type of information that is being presented and the audience that is to receive it.

(VoIP) Voice over Internet Protocol

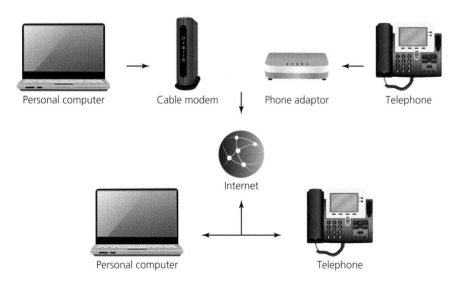

VoIP, or, in more common terms, phone service over the internet, is a technology used for the delivery of voice communications and multimedia sessions over Internet Protocol (IP) networks, such as the internet (using broadband internet connection).

It specifically refers to the provision of communications services (voice, fax, SMS, voice-messaging) over the public internet, rather than via the public switched telephone network (PSTN). This technology allows conversations to take place anywhere in the world as long as there is an internet connection.

Advantages	Disadvantages
Cost: As VoIP works off your internet connection, there is no need for a traditional phone line. Calls from PC to PC over the internet are free. Calls from PC to landline usually cost less than with a traditional phone line.	**Internet connection:** You cannot operate a VoIP phone system unless you have a reliable internet connection with sufficient bandwidth.
Accessibility: A VoIP phone system is distinctly different from a traditional phone system. Distance and location make no difference, whether you are calling your head office on the other side of the country or making a call to the other side of the world.	**Power problems:** If you operate a VoIP network and the power goes out, you no longer have an internet connection, so you no longer have access to your phone system. While this may be a minor irritation if it happens rarely and the outage is short, it can be a major headache if your power is out for a longer period.
Flexibility: With a private, internal phone network, you are limited to how many phones can be added to the system – with a VoIP network, you are limited only by bandwidth, so hundreds of connections can be made.	**Emergency services:** It can be difficult for the emergency services to trace calls to a VoIP system. Many businesses maintain at least one traditional phone line in order to allow communications at all times.
Extra features: VoIP comes with a wide selection of extra features such as call-forwarding, call-waiting, voicemail, caller ID, 3-way calling. Documents and pictures can be sent while engaging in conversation. It also allows video conversations to take place, accessing and exchanging data files, and more, while the conversation is ongoing. This allows for more effective and flexible meetings that can include people from multiple office locations throughout the world.	**Delay:** Due to bandwidth requirements, some calls may appear to lag, delay or disappear altogether. This problem is becoming less of an issue however, as newer, more sophisticated data algorithms come into use.

Activity

Look at the scenarios below – discuss in groups what method or methods you could use in these situations.

Or

On your own write out suggestions for each situation making justifications for the suggestions you have given.

A complaint has been received from a customer, highlighting that your team has not been following the correct company procedures. You have to remind staff of the requirements. In any one day, at least one member of staff may be out of the office or on holiday.

Following an audit by the Information Commissioner, your organisation has had to tighten up how it deals with data. Staff have all received training on data handling legislation, but staff have commented that they need a prompt to help them remember what they need to do in different circumstances.

A project you are working on has run into problems and you need to seek the advice of your team urgently. Some of your team members are in the office, but a number are working out of the office and you want to consult them all before you make a decision.

Exam-style questions practice

1   Describe methods of communication that could be used during induction training. (3 marks)
2   Compare written methods with face-to-face methods of communication. (3 marks)
3   Discuss the advantages and disadvantages of using electronic methods of communication. (6 marks)
4   Justify the use of an e-diary when an Administrative Assistant is arranging a formal meeting. (2 marks)
5   Compare the use of audio-conferencing with web-conferencing. (2 marks)

2 Making adjustments when communicating information to remove potential barriers

When planning communication it is important to consider what might stop people from understanding the message that is being transmitted – this will then allow the presenter or manager to make adjustments to make sure that the information is communicated as effectively as possible.

Lack of interest – there are a number of reasons why people lose interest when receiving information. This can be in a meeting, during a presentation or when reading information.

Meetings and presentations that last too long, where people are not active during the session, will lead to the audience losing focus – so a meeting or presentation that lasts for 2–3 hours isn't going to be successful without some variety to capture the audience. For example, something as simple as:

- giving a comfort break for 5–10 minutes
- having a group task/discussion to break up speeches
- limiting the amount of time people are just sitting and listening
- making sure that your presentation captures the audience.

The audience will lose interest if they are finding the information too difficult to understand or it could be that they already know about the topic and feel their time is being wasted. The presenter needs to understand their audience well and tailor the content of their presentation to make sure the audience stay with them.

People can also lose interest when reading information. Sometimes there is no way of getting away from reading a very long document but it can be made easier to follow by sticking to the point, making use of lists, diagrams and graphics to keep the reader engaged. This is not just limited to documents, it is also important to keep the information contained in emails and web pages concise and to the point. There is a lot of debate from web designers on whether users will scroll right to the end of the web page if the site is quite long – but ultimately if the audience is captured at the start, they will continue to read on.

Noise – if people cannot hear or are distracted by other people talking or general noise from other parts of the building, they will not be able to hear what is being said. It is important that in a large room, the presenter has a microphone so that everyone can hear from all parts of the room. If other people are talking, this may be because the presenter isn't holding their interest which results in others talking. Depending on the presenter or the audience members, someone might decide to ask them to be quiet. Everyone will have been somewhere trying to concentrate when people walk past the room making a lot of noise or they start digging up the road outside.

Some of these can be difficult to control but putting signs outside of rooms to alert people that a meeting is taking place, might help reduce passing noise or the venue might be aware of potential outside noise, particularly if it is planned building work and try to find a different room in the venue before the event starts. Also, making sure that the speaker has sound equipment will help make sure that their voice is not drowned out.

Jargon – information that contains lots of words and phrases that are very technical and require you to have specialist knowledge are useful in some cases but not if you are just hearing them for the first time. An expert who is delivering a presentation or creating documentation can easily forget that not everyone understands the terminology they are using and if they are not careful this can leave the target audience confused and ultimately they will stop paying attention or reading the information.

Note

There are many articles with details of research that has been carried out about the attention span of adults, ranging from 5 minutes up to 20 minutes.

Note

The Fold – web designers refer to above and below the fold. Above the fold is information that is visible as soon as you see the web page, what hooks the reader and below the fold is what the user has to scroll to see.

Note

The Plain English Campaign – www. plainenglish.co.uk/ – was established in 1979 to campaign and support organisations to simplify the language in their documents so everyone can understand what they are trying to say.

Technical difficulties – things go wrong and this will prevent the information from being shared. This could be:

- **Sound equipment** failing so people cannot hear.
- **Projector not working** so the audience cannot see the presentation or any video clips that were going to be shown.
- **Network failure** – email messages cannot be sent and received, video/web conference cannot take place, documents cannot be accessed that were going to be shown. Network failures are very rare these days, but it may be possible to continue a meeting or presentation if documents are printed or a discussion is needed. However, where technology was to be used to conduct the meeting, it will need to be postponed.
- **Loss of signal/loss of battery power** – as many people work while they are out of the office, it is possible that they may be in an area where there is no signal or if they have used their device all day, it may have finally run out of power.

It is often easy to overcome technical difficulties or to have a back-up plan so that the event can still take place, unless you are trying to communicate using the technology.

Language barriers – business is an international affair and it will not be uncommon to find presenters from other nations sharing their knowledge and expertise with a group. In the UK, we have a huge range of accents and some can be quite tricky to understand if you are not used to hearing them. Similarly, if someone is speaking in a language that is not their first language, this is a very daunting task for the speaker and can mean it may be difficult for a group of native speakers to understand everything that is being said. Support needs to be provided to make sure that any misunderstandings can be rectified – one of the organisers can step in and just ask for clarification on a point if they are on the ball with gauging the audience's interest levels.

Information overload – time is precious and organisations will want to make the most of the time that they have with their staff and this can lead to too much being crammed into presentations and meetings, which leaves staff feeling overwhelmed and leaving not remembering anything that was said. This is often the case when something new is being introduced or a member of staff is just starting a new job. The people organising meetings or presentations need to bear this in mind and make sure they try to avoid this situation – it may be that there has to be lots of shorter meetings to get the information across, or if there is only one opportunity to deliver the message, that there are support mechanisms in place in the form of leaflets, posters, discussions and meetings in teams to help make sure the information is received and understood.

Consequences of failure to remove potential barriers to communication

The meeting/presentation/event may need to be **postponed or cancelled** altogether if the speaker is not available for another date or another suitable date cannot be found to bring everyone together. This will mean that the information that was to be passed on was not received which could impact on people's ability to do their jobs. People will have had to waste their time getting to the event, meaning productivity has been lost for the organisation. There is also the possibility that if a venue had to be hired, money may have been wasted.

The people attending the event may become **agitated and frustrated** if there are problems and issues that are not resolved. This could result in people being unwilling to attend future events. If this is a staff training event and is something that happens frequently, staff may feel demotivated because of events not being carefully planned and prepared for. This could ultimately result in staff wanting to leave and cause problems for recruiting new staff if there is reputation for poor staff training. If these events are for customers, it could result in them choosing not to use your business because you have not presented a professional experience for them.

Some training has to take place because it is a **legal requirement** for the job. For example, people working with children must receive child protection training and staff dealing with personal information must receive data protection training – if this training is not completed this can result in fines and legal action being taken against the organisation.

Exam-style questions practice

6 Describe the barriers that may exist when communicating information to others. (3 marks)
7 Describe strategies that can be used to avoid the barriers that you provided in question 6. (3 marks)
8 Describe the consequences of possible communication barriers during a presentation with a large number of people in the audience. (4 marks)

Component 2 IT solutions for administrators

Chapter 4
Use of complex functions of a spreadsheet to support administrative tasks

What you should know

There are **two** topics to this chapter. By the end of this chapter you should be able to:

1 Complete a workbook, using complex functions and formulae.

2 Manipulate a workbook to aid analysis.

For your assessments and final assignment, you will be provided with spreadsheet workbooks, some of which could have two or three sheets populated with raw data – *i.e. no formulae, functions or consolidation applied*. It will be your problem-solving skills that will be required; therefore, the more you practise (quickly) inserting formulae and functions, and manipulating data, the more time you will have to think about the problem needing to be solved.

Before starting

Remember

For identification purposes on any classwork, assessment or final assignment, make sure your name + filename and tab name + gridlines and row and column headings fit on to one page landscape (select from the Page Layout > Page Setup). This can be done very easily – simultaneously on all sheets by grouping the sheets together.

- Group the required sheets – *Use the mouse pointer + Ctrl.* The sheets will go a pale colour and the active sheet will appear in bold.
- At the top of the screen check that **[Group]** has appeared after the filename.

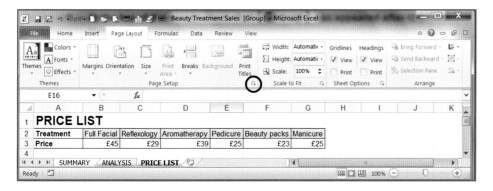

🖱 Select Page Setup. In each of the four Tabs select your preferences – but **ALWAYS** select the ones circled

Tab 1 – Page

Tab 2 – Margins

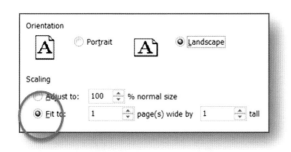

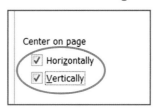

Tab 3 – Header/Footer

🖱 Select Custom Footer

In the Left Section Click on the two circled icons

- &[File] displays the File (Workbook) name

- &[Tab] displays the Sheet name being printed

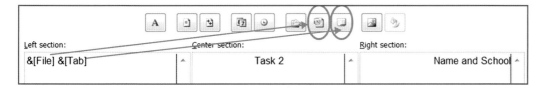

🖱 Click **OK** just once to return to **Tab 3**

Tab 4 – Sheet

It is probably a good idea to always select Gridlines and Row and column headings.

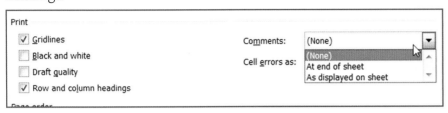

🖰 If they are not needed (and this will be a specific instruction) you can simply de-select for the specific printout.

🖰 You may be asked to show/display a comment(s) – select either option from the **Comments** section – make sure you know how to do this.

> Always de-select the grouping BEFORE proceeding with the task

The following examples use two spreadsheet workbooks[1] – **Beauty Treatment Sales** and **Wages** – *there are comments to help with completing them and some of the formulae is already done for you.*

1 Completing a workbook, using complex formulae and functions

A function is a predefined formula that calculates by using arguments in a specific way. An **argument** is a specific value in a function, *for example, it could be a range of cells.*

For example: =AVERAGE(B5:G5)

has **one** argument – *the range of cells from B5 through to G5.*

Functions are presented in categories to allow easy access for a beginner as well as expert users. The **Formula** Ribbon also has **Recently Used** and **AutoSum** shortcuts.

- **Recently Used** is very useful, as most users use the same functions that suit – on a regular basis.
- **AutoSum** is also available on the **Home** Ribbon.
- Selecting **fx** on the formula bar also gives access to the Functions.

Complex formulae – using the fx insert function

LOOKUP – V(ertical) and H(orizontal)

Use LOOKUP, in *the Lookup & Reference section of the Formulas Ribbon,* when you need to look in a single row or column and find a **value** from the same

(1) Go to www.hoddereducation.co.uk/updatesandextras

Remember

Use the function palette and the mouse to select the cells when composing a formula as it will avoid time-consuming keying in **and** saves making typo errors.

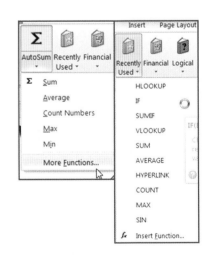

position in a second row or column. Most times the value you are looking up will be a price or an amount. For example, how many in stock; however, sometimes it will be a percentage that needs to be applied to a formula.

In the following example task, the price needs to be entered in the Current Price column. The data required are in a sheet named **Price List** in the form of two rows. Use HLOOKUP when the values you are looking for are located in rows across a table of data – *i.e. horizontally. Remember, using a function, rather than inserting the data one by one, means that any change in one piece of data will automatically be updated elsewhere.*

- Using the SS Workbook, **BEAUTY TREATMENT SALES**. Select the required sheet (**SALES**). (In this example, you are required to FIND AND INSERT, i.e. LookUp, the Price of each Treatment.)
- Select the correct cell (in this case D3).

In order to find this information and insert it in the required column:

- Select the correct cell (in this case D3).
- Click on the **fx** symbol on the formula bar – key-in or select HLOOKUP from the Insert Function dialogue box which pops up. (Alternatively you can select this from the Recently Used ▼ selection in the Formulas Ribbon.)
- The formula bar will now have =HLOOKUP() ready for you to make your selection.
- Use the mouse to select the information as required:
  - In the first box Lookup_value – click on Cell **B3** – this indicates what you are looking for – *in this case a text description.*
  - Click the Tab key to select Table_array – this indicates where the data are stored – can be in the same sheet or a separate sheet.
  - Use the mouse to select the PRICE LIST sheet and drag the mouse over cells B2:G3 – (Row 2 has the Lookup_value – i.e. the labels and Row 3 has the data you need – i.e. the prices). Click the F4 key to make the range absolute (i.e. it will not change when you fill down).
  - Click the Tab key again to select Row_Index_num. In this section key-in 2 – the prices are stored in the second row of the area selected (the fact that it is row 3 in the spreadsheet is irrelevant).
  - Click the Tab key again to select Range_lookup. In this section key-in False – because you want an exact match for each lookup value.

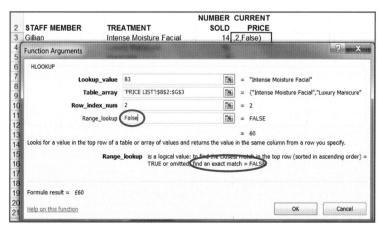

- Click OK and Fill down (for speed, double-click the bold black cross in the bottom right-hand corner of the cell D3 – very useful when replicating a column in a sheet with lots of rows).

Use VLOOKUP when the values you are looking for are located in a column in a table of data – i.e. vertically.

In this example shown:

🖱 Select the sheet named **Discounted SALES (V)**.

🖱 The same data required are in a sheet named **Prices** in the form of two columns.

🖱 The range A2:B8 has been named TREATMENT. (See section on named range function page 61.)

Conditional Statements – COUNTIF, SUMIF, SINGLE and MULTIPLE IF

COUNTIF

COUNTIF counts **How Many** cells in a range (E3:E12) containing a specific word, a specific value OR a value greater than, between, equal to, less than, etc. This is the condition 'IF' and would return a number (for example, 12) as an answer. It is fairly straightforward to use.

In a summary sheet it is sometimes required to Count some data in another sheet (see section on 3D formulae on page 65).

🖱 Using the SS Workbook, **WAGES** select the required sheet **WAGES SUMMARY**. (In this example, you are required to calculate how many staff are employed at each job level.)

🖱 Select the correct cell (in this case B10).

🖱 Select the COUNTIF Function Arguments palette from the Formulas Ribbon. In the Range section select the range of cells you want to search through (in this example the column containing Job Title). Because you will be replicating this, you need to lock this range by using the F4 key – this makes the range ABSOLUTE.

🖱 Select the COUNTIF Function Arguments palette from the **Formulas** Ribbon.

🖱 Use the Tab key to get to the next box and select the cell (A10) in the summary sheet containing the text you are looking for (the IF condition).

🖱 Fill down as required.

IF

The IF condition is used a lot in the Higher Assessments and Final Assessment – sometimes it is just a single condition – as the next example shows.

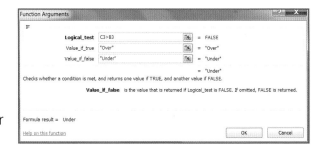

🖱 In the **WAGES SUMMARY** sheet, select cell D3 (to display whether the amount is Over or Under budget).

- Select the IF Function Arguments palette from the Formulas Ribbon.
- Using the mouse select the Logical_test: in this example C3>B3 (i.e. is one value higher or lower than another).
- Using the Tab key move to box 2 and key-in the Value_if_true (i.e. if it is greater, display the word shown – Over).
- Using the Tab key move to box 2 and key-in the Value_if_false (i.e. if it is less, display the word shown – Under).

SUMIF

SUMIF – use the SUMIF function to add the values in a range that meet the criteria that you specify. The function requires a REPEAT of the COUNTIF 'arguments', with an **extra** 'argument' requiring the addition of the numeric/currency field. This takes a bit more thought as follows:

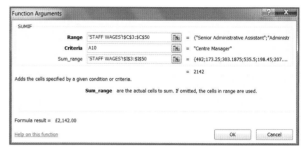

- In the **WAGES SUMMARY** sheet, select cell C10 (to calculate the total weekly wage per Job Level).
- Select the SUMIF Function Arguments palette from the Formulas ribbon.
- Repeat the steps above to get to the Criteria (IF condition).
- Use the Tab key to get to the third box.
- Using the mouse, select the same sheet (STAFF WAGES) and then select the range of cells you want to search through to add together (in the example to calculate the Total Wages for the job level specified).

Multiple IF – complex

Sometimes the criteria for an IF condition is quite complex. Imagine you are asked to calculate a bonus for staff dependent on the sales they have managed in a certain time. In the example the criteria is as follows.

Criteria – IF condition	Bonus to be applied
If sales are greater than £6000	Bonus due is 10% of sales
If sales are greater than £4000	Bonus due is 7.5% of sales
If sales are greater than £3000	Bonus due is 5% of sales

- Using the SS Workbook, **BEAUTY TREATMENT SALES**. Select the required sheet (**SUMMARY**).
- Select the correct cell (in this case C3).
- Select the IF Function Arguments palette from the **Formulas** ribbon.
- Using the mouse select the first criteria cell B3 and key-in >6000.
- Use the Tab key to get the next box and then select the cell B3 and key-in * 10%.
- Use the Tab key again BUT DON'T KEY ANYTHING IN, simply select IF in the Status bar and another new IF Function Arguments box will appear.

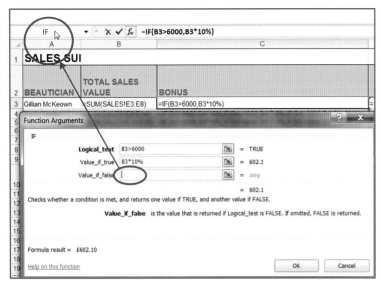

   Continue with the IF Functions Arguments palette until ALL three Criteria are selected and/or keyed in.

   The final value_if_false should include 0.

Remember

It is very important that the TAB key is used throughout this process. If you use the mouse, extra items appear in the formula (mainly the plus sign +) and it renders it useless and returns #VALUE in the cell – not a nice thing to see when you are trying to solve a problem.

The diagram below shows clearly the way a complex IF statement is constructed.

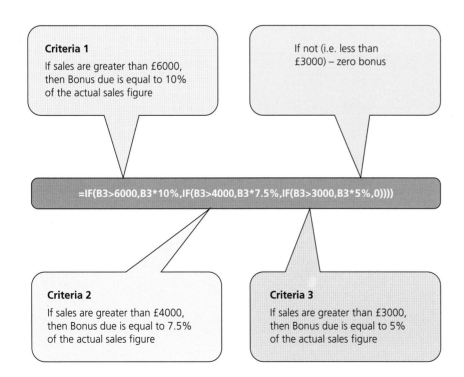

Criteria 1
If sales are greater than £6000, then Bonus due is equal to 10% of the actual sales figure

If not (i.e. less than £3000) – zero bonus

=IF(B3>6000,B3*10%,IF(B3>4000,B3*7.5%,IF(B3>3000,B3*5%,0))))

Criteria 2
If sales are greater than £4000, then Bonus due is equal to 7.5% of the actual sales figure

Criteria 3
If sales are greater than £3000, then Bonus due is equal to 5% of the actual sales figure

The IF statement must be hierarchical – which means

IF the criteria is > (greater than) you must begin with the highest value and work down

BUT

IF the criteria is < (less than) you must begin with the lowest value and work up

i.e.

>6000-comes BEFORE >4000-comes BEFORE >2500

ELSE – IF none of the criteria matches – 0 (zero)

The finished formulae should be as below:

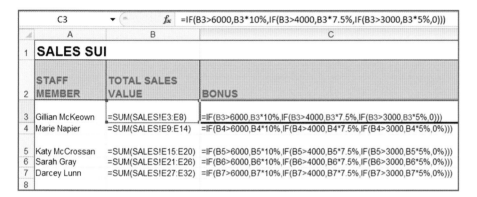

Combined arithmetic

This is probably the area where most students make the silliest of mistakes. There is not a safety net of a formula function dialogue box which points out any errors of syntax or if anything is missing from the formula when the OK is clicked. In most cases, the scenario requires you to calculate a percentage increase or decrease.

Task	Formula to key-in (use mouse to select cells)
Calculate a % increase – Hourly rate in cell C3 to be increased by 2.5%	=(C3*2.5%)+C3 i.e. Add 2.5% of the rate in cell C3 to the rate in cell C3 – the brackets () are optional but it makes it a bit easier to understand.
Calculate a % decrease – Price in cell C3 to be decreased by 2.5%	=C3 –(C3*2.5%) i.e. from the price in cell C3 less (subtract) 2.5% of the price in cell C3 – the brackets () are optional but it makes it a bit easier to understand.
Calculate a percentage increase (in a price or a rate) incorporating a V-HLOOKUP – Percentage increase data are stored in a separate (columnar) table so the formula has to do that first, THEN calculate the percentage increase and THEN add it to the original data – gets easier with practice!	=VLOOKUP(C3,Increase_rate,2,false)*C3+C3 i.e. from the Increase data in the separate table, the lookup finds the percentage increase, and multiplies it by the value in cell C3 and ADDS it to the original value in C3. For example: £10 plus a % of £10. No need to key-in the brackets as they are entered with the Insert Function data dialogue box.
Multiply one value by another value	=D3*B3 i.e. multiply one value by another – e.g. Hourly Rate x Hours Worked

Roundup/down

This is a function to either round a calculation up or down – i.e. usually to the nearest 0, 1 or 2 decimal places. The software will automatically round up, if more than half (0.5) and round down if less than half. Another way is to format cells for 0, 1 or 2 places.

The **Roundup** and **Rounddown** function is often used by an organisation when calculating a price and hourly rates of pay. When calculating a price it is normal to round down (the customer benefits) and when calculating a cost round up is often used.

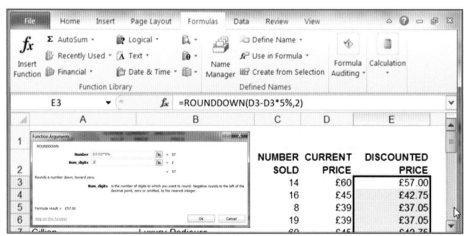

🖱 Using the SS Workbook, **BEAUTY TREATMENT SALES**. Select the required sheet **Discount SALES (V)**.

🖱 Select the correct cell (in this case E3).

In the example arithmetic formula, ROUNDDOWN is being used to make the price more attractive, i.e. to reduce (discount) the price by 5 per cent; rounding up would make the price slightly higher.

Complex functions

Working with Named Cells and Ranges of Cells

Naming cells is covered in National 5 Administration and IT and is very useful when absolute formula is required – it makes formulae easier to understand too. The same function can be applied to a range of cells, e.g. a Price List. Naming a cell makes Lookups and 3D formula very easy to do and understand. The function is the same for naming a range using Name Manager² as follows:

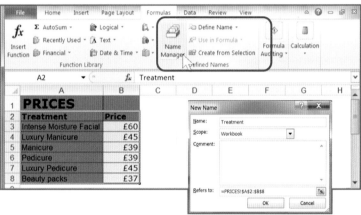

🖱 Select the range of cells you want to Name.

🖱 Select Name Manager and click on New in the pop-up dialogue box.

🖱 No need to enter a name as the suggested name – *from the first cell of the range* – is fit for the purpose. Saves time keying-in anyway.

Conditional cell formatting

Sometimes it's hard to read and interpret data by scanning rows and rows of information. But you can use conditional formatting to make certain data stand out, helping you to analyse data, and to identify patterns and trends using colour, bold, italics, underline, etc. (i.e. **formatting**!). By applying conditional formatting to your data, you can easily and quickly identify variances in a range of values with a quick glance.

This can be applied as follows: use the **WAGES** workbook **WAGES SUMMARY** sheet.

🖱 Use the mouse to select the cell range that you want to format (D3:D6).

🖱 Select **Conditional Formatting** from the Home Ribbon Styles section.

🖱 Select **Manage Rules** option – you need this option as it will give you more control to follow instructions and add more than one condition.

🖱 Select **New Rule** from the Rules Manager dialogue box.

---

(2) E-file Beauty Treatment Sales – this has already been applied

🖰 In the Select a Rule Type options select – **Format only cells that contain.**

🖰 In the Edit Rule Description options (middle box), select the comparison operator – in this case **equal to.**

🖰 In the third box, key-in **Over.**

🖰 Now click on the **Format** button and change the font to **Bold** *Italics*, and Red colour font. Click OK twice – yes twice!

This will bring up another Rules Manager box.

🖰 Select **New Rule** again and repeat the steps – except – change the font to **Bold**, Blue colour font.

🖰 Click the **Apply** button.

The **Rules Manager** should look like this – if it doesn't – do it again – you have missed something – honestly, you have!

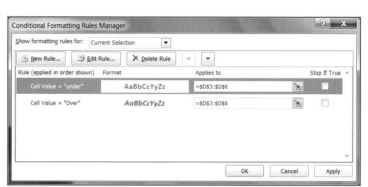

Filters

By filtering information in a worksheet, you can find values quickly. You can filter on one or more columns of data. With filtering, you can control not only what you want to see, but what you want to exclude. You can filter based on choices you make from a list, or you can create specific filters to focus on exactly the data that you want to see. You can search for text and numbers when you filter by using the **Search** box in the filter interface. When you filter data, entire rows are hidden if values in one or more columns don't meet the filtering criteria. You can filter on numeric or text values, or filter by colour for cells that have colour formatting applied to their background or text.

Applying filters to complex data

This example is for illustration only and uses the **STAFF WAGES** sheet in the **WAGES** workbook.

- From the Data Ribbon, select Filter – this is a toggle key (to remove Filters simply click again).
- Every Column Heading (Field) now displays ▼.
- Clicking on this will display various options.

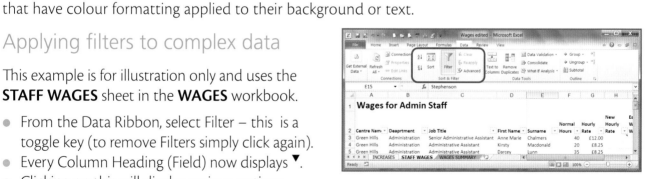

Using filters to simplify formula

For example; if, in the example shown, all Centre Managers were to receive an increased hourly rate – by filtering for the Job Title Field, the hourly rate could be changed quite easily and filled down – no need for an IF statement.

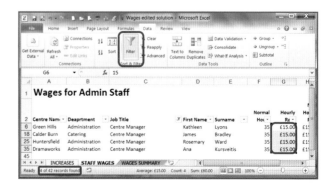

Sorting on more than one criteria

This example uses the **WAGES SUMMARY**
sheet in the **WAGES** workbook.

From the **Data** Ribbon, **Editing** section, select
Sort in the **Sort & Filter** section OR use the
Custom Sort option from the **Sort & Filter** ▼ option in the **Home** Ribbon.

Hints & tips

*Click the mouse anywhere
within the data – no need
to manually select if there
is only one main heading.*

Remember

*Take care with sorting data in a spreadsheet. Unlike a database
where all the information in a "row" is actually a complete record,
using the A to Z shortcut can lead to just ONE column being
sorted and making a complete nonsense of the rest of the data.*

In the example shown, the Sort is done using the **Sort** Option as follows:
- Select Under/Over Budget ▼ from the Sort by
pull-down options menu.

The Default Order is A to Z ▼ (Largest to smallest
if number value) – this is easily changed in the
pull-down menu.

When sorting on more than one criteria/column:
- Select **Add Level** from the Sort dialogue box.
- Select the next column to be sorted (in the
example shown it is the column containing the
names of the Centres).
- Repeat the process as often as required.

Because the box has the Data Header box ticked, the software recognises
not to include the column (field) headings in the sort.

Individual sorts can be removed by selecting X **Delete Level**.

Sorting horizontally by rows[3]

This example is for illustration only and refers to
the **PRICE LIST** sheet in the **BEAUTY TREATMENT
SALES** workbook.
- Select the Data to be sorted (it is quicker with
horizontal sorting) and open the Custom sort
Dialogue Box.

(3) This has already been done in the e-file.

- Select Options from the **Sort dialogue box**.
- Change the default from Sort top to bottom to Sort left to right. Click OK.
- Select criteria as needed – in this case row 2. Click OK.
- The data columns **B** to **G** will now be sorted horizontally.

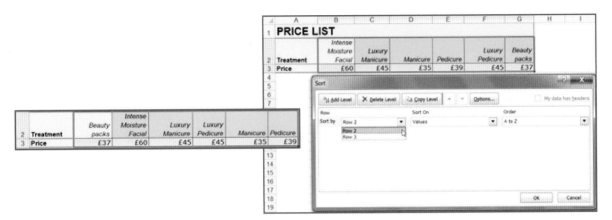

Comments

You can add notes to a worksheet by using comments. Using comments can help you make a worksheet easier to understand by providing additional context for the data it contains. For example, you can use a comment as a note that provides information about data in an individual cell. You can also add a comment to a column heading to provide guidance on data that a user should enter. When a cell has a comment, a red indicator appears in the corner of the cell. When you rest the pointer on the cell, the comment appears.

You can display or hide them and when you no longer need them, you can delete them.

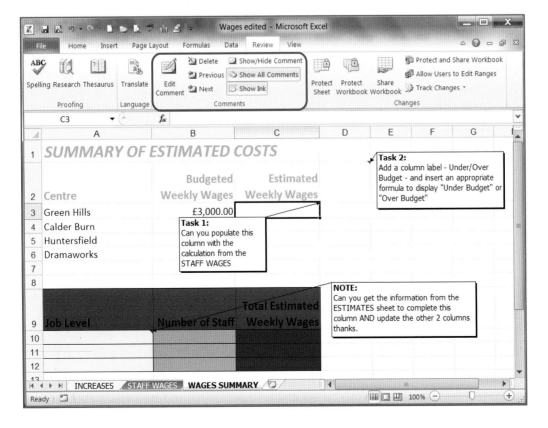

2 Manipulating a workbook to aid analysis

Data consolidation: summary sheets – 3D formulae

To summarise and display results from data on separate worksheets you can consolidate the data from each separate worksheet into one worksheet, for example, a **chart** or use of a **summary sheet** (using 3D formulae).

> ### 3D formulae
>
> 3D formula makes reference to data on another sheet and is indicated by an exclamation mark after the name of the sheet (e.g. SALES!).
>
> Simply put this means that if the sheets were printed, the summary sheet would be on top of the pile and the data transferred to the summary sheet would be on the sheets below – three dimensional.

The worksheets you consolidate can be in the same workbook as the chart/summary worksheet or in other workbooks. When you consolidate data in one worksheet, you can more easily update/edit it.

Apart from charts, the most common data consolidation method in administration tasks is the use of summary sheets to transfer totals and averages. However, COUNT, COUNTIF and SUMIF are also widely used.

- Using the SS Workbook, **BEAUTY TREATMENT SALES**. Select the required sheet (**SUMMARY**).
- Select the correct cell (*in this case B3*).

In the example shown SUM function is used to calculate the total sales per person (total the range for that person).

Note that the SUM function cannot be filled down (different ranges selected) so no need for absolute cell references. Each calculation (SUM) is individually applied.

	A	B	C
1	SALES SUMMARY		
2	BEAUTICIAN	TOTAL SALES VALUE	TOTAL SALES
3	Gillian McKeown	=SUM(SALES!E3:E8)	=SUM(SALES!C3:C8)
4	Marie Napier	=SUM(SALES!E9:E14)	=SUM(SALES!C9:C14)
5	Katy McCrossan	=SUM(SALES!E15:E20)	=SUM(SALES!C15:C20)
6	Sarah Gray	=SUM(SALES!E21:E26)	=SUM(SALES!C20:C25)
7	Darcey Lunn	=SUM(SALES!E27:E32)	=SUM(SALES!C27:C32)
8			

The same could be applied to other simple formulae functions – *Average, Minimum, Maximum, Count etc.*

However, the more complex SUMIF function is used to look for something – *criteria* – and then total the range in another column. In this instance it is **essential** that absolute cell references are used (*or the range will change every fill down*) either by locking the cells with the F4 key function (&C&4, etc.) or by naming the range.

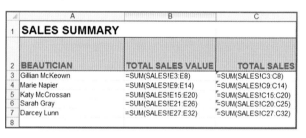

TREATMENTS	TOTAL NUMBER	TOTAL VALUE
Intense Moisture Facial	=SUMIF(SALES!$B$3:$B$32,E3,SALES!$C$3:$C$32)	=SUMIF(SALES!$B$3:$B$32,E3,SALES!$E$3:$E$32)
Luxury Manicure	=SUMIF(SALES!$B$3:$B$32,E4,SALES!$C$3:$C$32)	=SUMIF(SALES!$B$3:$B$32,E4,SALES!$E$3:$E$32)
Manicure	=SUMIF(SALES!$B$3:$B$32,E5,SALES!$C$3:$C$32)	=SUMIF(SALES!$B$3:$B$32,E5,SALES!$E$3:$E$32)
Pedicure	=SUMIF(SALES!$B$3:$B$32,E6,SALES!$C$3:$C$32)	=SUMIF(SALES!$B$3:$B$32,E6,SALES!$E$3:$E$32)
Luxury Pedicure	=SUMIF(SALES!$B$3:$B$32,E7,SALES!$C$3:$C$32)	=SUMIF(SALES!$B$3:$B$32,E7,SALES!$E$3:$E$32)
Beauty packs	=SUMIF(SALES!$B$3:$B$32,E8,SALES!$C$3:$C$32)	=SUMIF(SALES!$B$3:$B$32,E8,SALES!$E$3:$E$32)

Sometimes 3D formula is easier done using sub-totals (see section on grouping, pages 67–68).

Pivot tables

When a Workbook contains a lot of data, a very good way to analyse/ view these data is by using a **pivot table**. This is an interactive worksheet table created so that large amounts of data can be quickly summarised, organised and compared. The data used to create such a table is called the **source data**. This can come from spreadsheet data or from a table created in a database file.

The pivot table has its name because data can be rotated – using the row and column headings to give different configurations of the data. If the source data changes or is updated, the table updates (just like a chart would update).

To specify which portion of the source data to use in a pivot table, you choose fields and items. Fields are categories of data and items are subcategories in a field (e.g. 2019 would be an item in a field called Year).

Note

There are two types of fields:

* Row/column/page fields which usually contain a limited set of text values, e.g. North, South, East, West.
* Data fields which usually contain numeric data (quite a lot of data) used for aggregating (SUM, AVERAGE, COUNT, etc.) e.g. Sales figures, etc.

🖰 Using the SS Workbook, **BEAUTY TREATMENT SALES**. Select the required sheet **(SALES)**.

🖰 Click anywhere in the data to be summarised – no need to select the data as it is all being used.

🖰 From the Insert Ribbon, select Pivot Table.

🖰 A Source Data dialogue box will pop-up showing all of the data selected (just like a chart) – click OK.

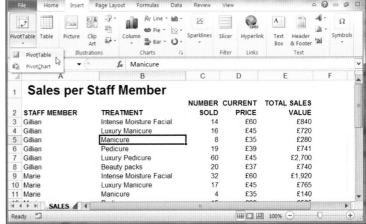

A new sheet is automatically created – it can be renamed with an appropriate name.

The Pivot Table Field List will appear – this is when you have to THINK about what you want to summarise – *see information above referring to field types.*

For the purposes of the example shown, the fields required AND selected are as follows:

Main Report Filter – Select Member of Staff Field – drag as requested.

Row Labels – Select Treatment (the default will show Row Labels – change this in the formula box to TREATMENT).

Values – Using the mouse, drag BOTH Total Sales Field and Total Value Sales Field into this area. Rename the Fields as shown on page 67 – see completed sheet.

You will need to format the cells (for currency where required) and adjust the columns to wrap and right align text headings. This can be done in the Number format option in the Pivot Table dialogue box but just as easily by using the normal spreadsheet formatting ribbon.

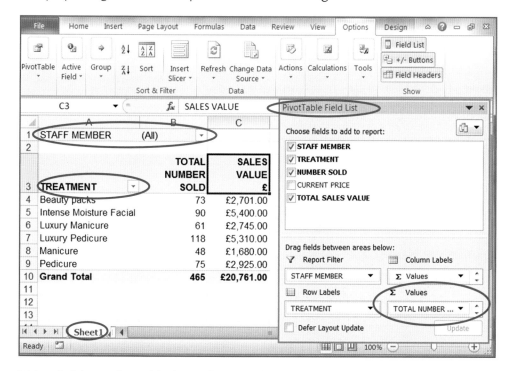

Value fields can be added or edited to display average, minimum, maximum, etc. using the Value Field Settings from the pull down menu in the value field.

The data can now be viewed:

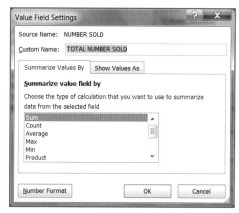

- *by Staff Member* – use the filter ▼ shortcut on the main report field.
- *by Treatment* – use the filter ▼ shortcut on the row field.

OR

- *pivoted* to display and view – *treatment* as the main report field, and *Staff Member* as the Row Labels field. This can be done by using the mouse to drag and swap the fields on the Pivot Table Field List dialogue box.

Grouping (Outline) using Subtotal function

If you have a list of data that you want to group, i.e. summarise (displaying Subtotals – Sum, Average, Min, Max, etc.), you can create a group/outline of up to eight levels. You can automatically calculate **subtotals** and **grand totals** in a list for a column by using the Subtotal command.

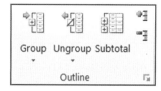

 Note

The Subtotal command will appear greyed out (i.e. unavailable) if you are working with a completely unsorted Sheet. To add subtotals in a table, you must first convert the table to a normal or sorted range of data – i.e. in some sort of grouped fashion.

Subtotals are calculated with a summary function, such as Sum or Average. You can display more than one type of summary function for each column.

Grand totals are derived from detail data, *not from the values in the subtotals*. For example, if you use the Average summary function, the grand total row displays an average of all of the detail rows in the list, *i.e. it does not include the values in the subtotal rows*.

Applying grouping to large amounts of data can also be very useful when transferring totals, etc. (dynamically using formulae) to a summary sheet.

To apply Grouping using subtotals:

🖱 Using the SS Workbook, **WAGES**, select the required sheet (**STAFF WAGES**).

🖱 Click anywhere in the data.

🖱 From the **Data** Ribbon select **Subtotals** in the Outline section.

🖱 Select Hours per Week and Weekly Wage – to show the SUM subtotal at each change in Centre Name click OK.

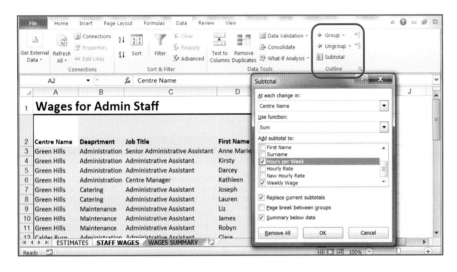

The data will now have Totals at the end of each Centre and a Grand total at the very bottom of the data.

To add other functions, such as Average, follow the same procedure *except* –

🖱 Select Average from the Use function box.

🖱 **De-select** the Replace current subtotals – if you don't do this you will lose all of the previously applied SUM subtotals.

This can be repeated as often as required.

The final version can also be viewed at different groupings/outline by selecting one of the numbers at the top left-hand side of the sheet – this version is level 3.

These levels can be easily transferred to a summary sheet using 3D formula. It is a good idea to quickly **Hide** the columns not required – in this example **B-E** and **G-H**.

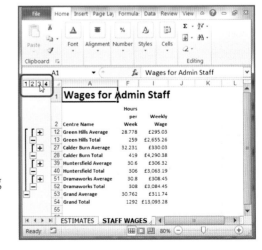

The formula to transfer the total weekly wage would, therefore, be (using the mouse to select the sheet and cell) for example:
=STAFFWAGES!I13

> If you can practise, practise, practise all of these functions, formatting and formulae (using this book as a reference), you should be well on your way to doing very well in the spreadsheet sections of your Assessments and final Assignment.

Finally

When worksheets contain large amounts of data, it is sometimes very difficult to view all of the information contained in the sheet – reducing the percentage view can make the information too small to read! Scrolling down to see more information on the screen, means that the Column Headings (i.e. Fields) disappear. This can be easily avoided by locking parts of the sheet table so that they remain visible, while the rest of the worksheet scrolls. The formatting required is Freeze Panes.

To apply Freeze Panes:

- Place the cursor in the leftmost cell BELOW the Headings you want to lock.
- Select **Freeze Panes** ▼ from the **View Ribbon**, Window Section.
- Select the First Option – Freeze Panes – keep rows and columns visible while scrolling.

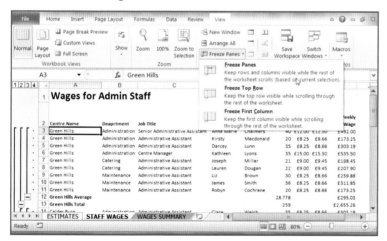

- To unfreeze – simply select that option from the **Freeze Panes** ▼ menu.

Chapter 5

Use of complex functions of a database to support administrative tasks

What you should know

There are **three** topics to this chapter. By the end of this chapter you should be able to:

1 Create relationships between tables in a database.
2 Manipulate the database using advanced functions.
3 Create a database report.

Database: revision

The main reason you spend time entering all of your data into an electronic database is so that you can easily **find** and **work** with the information. It is, therefore, essential that detailed planning is done when designing a database for use in any Administrative function.

- **Data** are the **values** that you store in the database.
- **Information** is data that you **retrieve** from the database in some meaningful and useful way.

Once the database has been designed and built **Queries**, **Forms** and **Reports** can be designed and created to:

- allow data to be input (**Forms**)
- retrieve and print information from it (**Queries** and **Reports**).

One of the main aims of good database design is to remove duplicated data. The principles of a good database design can be summarised as follows:

- One table, one subject.
- One field, one value.
- One table, one primary key.

Once the tables are designed to contain just the right amount and type of data, it is then that they can be joined – this is when the database becomes a relational database.

Types of fields – additional information

Memo field	<ul><li>When this is selected from the Data Type options, text and numbers can be entered – useful for large amounts of descriptive text.</li><li>Best searched using the wildcard function – more of this later.</li></ul>
AutoNumber	<ul><li>When this is selected from the Data Type options, a unique sequential number (i.e. incremented by 1) or random numbers are assigned whenever a new record is added to a table.</li><li>AutoNumbers can't be repeated and, in fact, when deleted cannot appear again.</li><li>The default Primary Key – i.e. when prompted for a primary key when creating a new table – is in the form of AutoNumber.</li></ul>

1 Relational database

- A relational database consists of a collection of data organised into tables. Tables are **linked** together by defining relationships between them.
- These relationships are based on the tables having a **common field**, and they allow you to **bring together** data from different tables.

A relationship in a database is, therefore, a connection between two tables that allows them to share data and is based on the tables having one field in common.

What is a valid relationship?

The two tables must have a common field so that Access® can **match** values in those fields when joining the tables. It is better if both fields have the same name – although not necessary.

One field is called the **primary** key and the related field is called the **foreign** key. To allow the database to identify these fields, the creator of the database must allocate a **primary** key to the field in the first table (i.e. to the **unique** piece of data about the Record – like an Employee Number) and in the second table the field which contains similar (but not unique) data – called the foreign key. The primary key is identified by the key icon.

Primary Key

The **common** fields must have the same data type. For example: a **text** field to a **text** field, a **number** field to a **number** field, etc.

In the example below each record in the **Staff** table (giving details about the employee) has a related record in the **Sales** table (giving details about the sales made by the employee) and a related record in the **Stock** table (giving details about the stock sold).

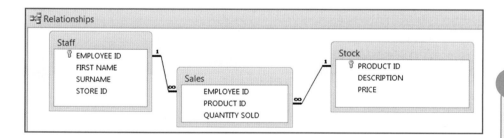

The primary key in the Staff table is **EMPLOYEE ID** (the unique information assigned to each member of staff).

The primary key in the Stock table is **PRODUCT ID** (the unique information assigned to each item of stock).

The foreign keys in the Sales table are **EMPLOYEE ID** and **PRODUCT ID** (the link between the two tables – who sold what).

By creating a relationship between the tables, the database can search for the sales made by any employee using the EMPLOYEE ID – OR search for information on who sold a particular item of stock using the PRODUCT ID.

Types of relationships

- **One-to-many** (shown by the ∞ infinity symbol beside the foreign key) relationship is one in which each record in the first table can have MANY matching records in the second table. But each record in the second table can have only ONE matching record in the first table. In the sample shown one member of staff can make many sales.
- **One-to-one** (shown by the 1 beside both primary keys) relationship is where each record in one table can only have ONE matching record in the second table and vice versa.
- **Many-to-many** – this is where a third table – sometimes called a junction table – breaks down the one to **many** relationship in two other (one to many) tables. In the sample one employee can sell **many** different products and one product can be sold by many employees.
- **Referential integrity** – a set of rules that ensures that the relationship between records in related tables are valid, and that you do not accidentally delete or change related data.
- **Cascade Update Related fields** – when this is selected, if you change a primary key VALUE in the primary table, Access automatically changes any matching values in related records.
- **Cascade Delete Related fields** – when this is selected, if you delete a record in the primary table, Access automatically deletes all matching records in the related table.
- **Cascades work in one direction only** – changes to the primary table are automatically applied to the related table but not vice versa.

Creating and printing a relationship

The first thing that needs to be done is to set the primary keys for each table. Remember that although not all tables need a primary key to connect with other tables, it is better to set a primary key to every table. The procedure to follow is:

- Open the tables in **Design** mode.
- Set the field containing the unique information. For example, if you set Employee ID to a **primary** key, there are no duplicates possible.
- Close **Design** mode by selecting the **Datasheet View** from the pull-down menu. At this point you will be prompted to Save – select YES.

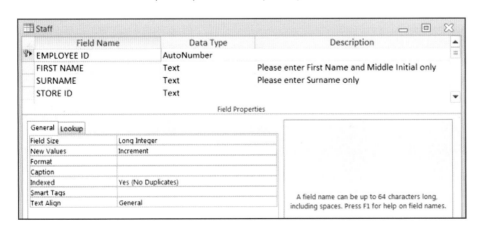

Repeat this for the other tables (*you may have to create a Primary key field – the default is AutoNumber*).

Once the tables have each been allocated with a primary key, the relationships can be created by linking the Primary key to the Foreign key (*and/or edited as required*).

From the **Database Tools** Ribbon select – **Relationships** from the same named section. The Relationship Tools Ribbon will appear. (If the tables do not appear automatically, select **Show Table** on the Ribbon in the **Relationships** section.)

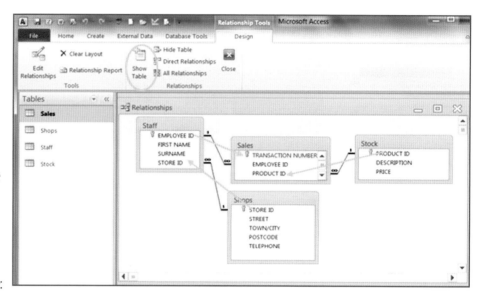

Using the mouse, drag the Primary Key field to the corresponding (foreign) field in another table, for example:

Staff Table Primary key EMPLOYEE ID -> Sales Table Foreign key EMPLOYEE ID

Shops Table Primary key STORE ID -> Staff Table Foreign key STORE ID

Stock Table Primary key PRODUCT ID -> Sales Table Foreign key PRODUCT ID

Sales Table: although it has a primary key TRANSACTION NUMBER it does not have a corresponding foreign key – therefore no relationship can be created.

Remember to enforce Referential integrity or the relationship will be undefined (i.e. will not show the ∞ symbol but a thin indeterminate line).

- One Shop has or can have MORE THAN ONE (many) Staff.
- One member of Staff can have MORE THAN ONE (many) Sales.
- One Product can have MORE THAN ONE (many) Sales.
- One member of Staff can sell MORE THAN ONE (many) Product.

- To Print the Relationships, select **Relationship Report** from the **Tools** Section of the **Relationship Tools** Ribbon. The report will automatically generate itself and appear.
- In design view edit the report – add your name in the footer and remove the date from the header (hint – select the label with the mouse and press the Delete key – not the backspace) – remember use the Label **Aa** option from the Controls ▾ menu in the Design Ribbon of the **Report Design Tools.**

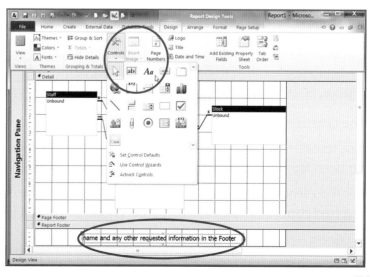

- Key-in your name, etc. and then it is a good idea to format the text for Black (Automatic) and at least 12 pt font size.
- Rather than resizing individual boxes to fit the page change to **landscape** using the **Page Setup** Ribbon.
- Change to Print Preview to check everything is visible.
- The finished report is now ready to send to the printer.

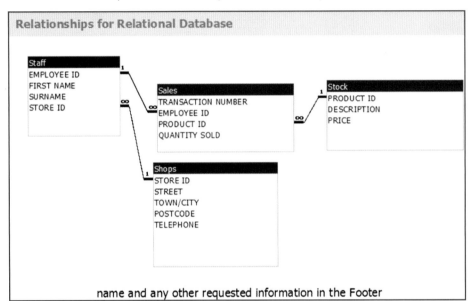

2 Manipulating the database using advanced functions

Search using Not, Or and a Wildcard

A typical example of a search in an assessment or assignment would be as follows:

'Find information about our Diamond and Ruby packages provided by Ninian Travel Company for all our customers – except our Paisley ones who have already been contacted'

The criteria is very simple and would require the use of three tables from the database and the following search criteria:

Table	Field	Criteria	Using
CUSTOMERS	TOWN	all except Paisley	Not Paisley
DETAILS	TYPE OF PACKAGE	only Diamond or Ruby packages	Diamond or Ruby
TRAVEL AGENTS	NAME	Ninian Travel	Ninian*

The criteria is very simple:

Not represented by <> – however, you can simply key-in the word not – no need for <> as the database automatically changes it.

OR represented by "xxx" OR "yyy" (i.e. either/or) – no need to key in the inverted commas ("") for the actual criteria and no need for capitals for or.

Wildcard – represented by Like "" – no need to key-in Like "" you can simply insert an asterisk either before or after the key word, for example, Ninian*.

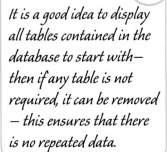

Hints & tips

It is a good idea to display all tables contained in the database to start with— then if any table is not required, it can be removed — this ensures that there is no repeated data.

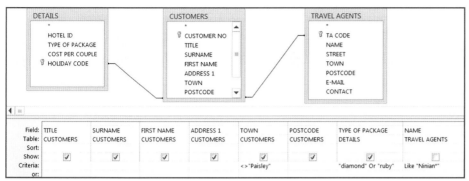

Note !

With the exception of Wildcards when keying-in criteria – simply key-in the normal word, for example, not, or, and the software will automatically change it to the proper syntax, that is, no need for inverted commas "", capital letters, date formats #, not, between, etc.

Once the **TAB** key or **RETURN/ENTER** key is pressed, the syntax will appear.

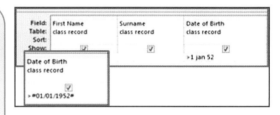

Using aggregate functions in a query

Σ Totals

Note !

In order to apply aggregates, care has to be taken that not too many fields are selected, as this does not allow Σ Totals (i.e. Grouping repeated data) to be successfully applied.

Count calculates 'how many'

In this example, you have been asked to Count the number of Staff per Shop. The Fields required come from two tables – Staff and Shops – no other table is required.

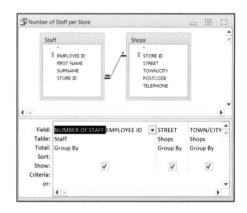

- The fields required are – EMPLOYEE ID (from the Staff Table) and STREET and TOWN/CITY (from the Shops Table).
- Click on Σ Totals in the Query Tools Design Ribbon.
- A new row appears – Total: Group By.
- From the Group By ▾ pull down menu select Count.
- Rename the field (key-in NUMBER OF STAFF: in front of the field name – use a colon to separate this from the field label – don't delete the field label).

 The result of the Query (Count) can then be printed by exporting to a Word document or saved and used for a report.

Run

NUMBER OF STAFF	STREET	TOWN/CITY
2	1 Main Street	Aberdeen
2	1 South Union Street	Edinburgh
2	234 Cathcart Road	Glasgow
1	4 Carnegie Street	Dundee
2	5 Maryhill Drive	Glasgow
1	90 High Street	Glasgow

Remember

The Field label can also be edited in Report and Word Table format.

Sum (Total), Average, Minimum and Maximum can all be done using the same procedure, i.e. using ∑ Totals in the Query Design AND selecting the (*Aggregate*) Function required from the Total: ▼Pull-down Menu.

This particular example also has Sort:Ascending applied to the Total items Sold (this is lowest number to highest)

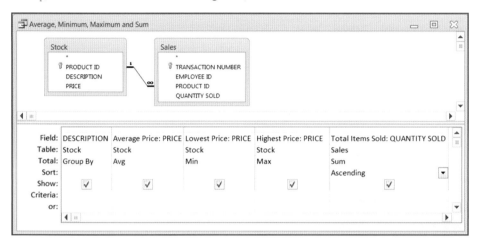

Using calculated fields in queries

Calculated field is a field that displays the result of a calculation using other fields in the Query.

E.g. a calculated field named – New Price – could calculate the increased/decreased price by using the expression shown.

You create a calculated field by keying-in the:
- Field name (REDUCED PRICE:) and
- the required calculation in the field row ([PRICE])*0.9)

    i.e. multiply the number in the Price field by 0.9 to reduce the price by 10%

Calculations (Expressions) can include one or more of the following:

Arithmetic operators – (add +, subtract –, multiply*, divide /)
Aggregates – Sum(Field), Average(Field), Count(Field).

The following table shows some examples of custom calculations.

Expression	Result
[Quantity]*[Unit Price]	Calculates the total cost of something by multiplying the unit price by the quantity in stock (or ordered)
[Unit Price]*.95	Discounts the Unit Price by 5%
[Class Fee]*[Class Max]	Calculates the Maximum Income possible
<Date()-30	Selects records where the date is more than 30 days earlier than the current date

It is essential that the syntax of the Expression is correct – any errors/extra/missing characters will result in an error message.
- Field names must be enclosed within square brackets [Name].
- Expressions being evaluated by a function (for example: Sum) are better being enclosed in parentheses (round brackets).

Remember you must select the 'Show' check box in the column/field in the 'Total' row.

The calculated field must be formatted appropriately – Right-click on the column and select Properties from the pop-up menu (Currency 2 decimal places).

Microsoft Access ✕

ⓘ **The expression you entered contains invalid syntax.**

You omitted an operand or operator, you entered an invalid character or comma, or you entered text without surrounding it in quotation marks.

[OK] [Help]

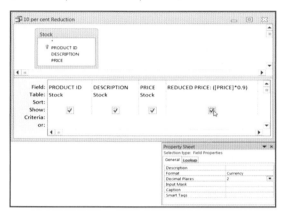

The final calculated query should look like this:

PRODUCT ID	DESCRIPTION	PRICE	REDUCED PRICE
ARM2378	Armchair	£299	£269.10
ARM2456	Armchair	£399	£359.10
OCC123	Small Table	£125	£112.50
OCC789	Nest of Tables	£235	£211.50
SB1234	Sofabed	£259	£233.10
SB3254	Sofabed	£399	£359.10
SO268	3-seater sofa	£499	£449.10
SO378	2-seater sofa	£299	£269.10
TA123	Table with 6 chairs	£999	£899.10
TA236	Table with 4 chairs	£799	£719.10

Activity

Copy this table and create (write) the Calculation Expression.

Field name – *calculation required*	Calculation required = use proper syntax
Class Fee **to be reduced by 10%**	
Class Fee **to be reduced by 2.5%**	
Class Fee **to be reduced by 12.5%**	
Class Fee **to be increased by 10%**	
Class Fee **to be increased by 2.5%**	
Class Fee **to be increased by 12.5%**	
Price **to be increased by 15%**	
Discount **of 15% due on Amount Owing**	

Note !

* If you can't get your head round DB calculations you can do the calculation on a spreadsheet (Exporting to Excel®) and then copy back into the DB if it is needed for a report using Paste Append from the Paste ▾ menu.

* If it is not needed for a report simply print straight from the spreadsheet.

Using Advanced Filter/Sort

When data have to be sorted on more than one field:

- Select the **Advanced Filter/Sort** option from the Sort & Filter section of the Home Ribbon.

- (*The dialogue box will look like a normal query in Design View.*) Select the fields IN THE ORDER REQUIRED.
- Select the sorting required – Ascending (alphabetical order or smallest to largest) or Descending (reverse alphabetical order or largest to smallest).
- To display sorted data simply Toggle Filter.
- The Advanced Sort can be saved if required.

Working with forms

Creating a form for inputting data using more than one table

A **form** is a database object that you can use to create an interface that is directly connected to a data source such as a table. The form can be used to enter, edit, or display data from that data source. To be more selective about what fields appear on a form, you can use the 'Form Wizard'. You can also use fields from more than one table as long as you specified the relationships between the tables beforehand.

A typical example required in an Assessment or Assignment would be:

> Create a Database Form to allow Sales to be entered easily using the following Fields:
>
> - EMPLOYEE ID, PRODUCT ID, DESCRIPTION, QUANTITY SOLD, TOWN/CITY, STREET. Note – the fields all come from different tables.
>
> Enhance the form:
>
> - with a graphic in the form header, and
> - a message in the form footer as follows, 'enter all sales data and check accuracy before confirming'.
> - Print one record only.

- On the **Create** tab, in the **Forms** group, click **Form Wizard**.
- From the first page select the fields required, i.e. from the **Sales** Table select EMPLOYEE ID, PRODUCT ID, DESCRIPTION and QUANTITY SOLD.
- Do not click **Next** or **Finish**. Instead, select another table (Shops) from the pull down menu and click on all fields that you want to include on the form, i.e. TOWN/CITY and **STREET**. Click **Next**.

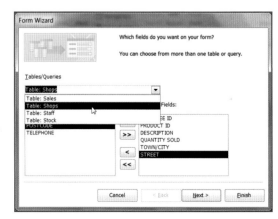

- On the next page, the wizard prompts for Grouping – not necessary in this case.
- On the next page, the wizard prompts for layout choice. It's best to choose Columnar format – Tabular just looks like a single line of a table.
- On the last page of the wizard, it suggests a name for the form – it will show the name of the first table selected – in this case Sales. As this is a suitable name, click **Finish**.
- The form header will also be automatically generated as the name of the first table selected – **Sales**.

Improving the appearance of a form

Once the form is generated, changes can be made by selecting **Design View**.

Font type, size, colour, etc. can be changed easily, use *Select All (Ctrl A) to change all at the same time*. If individual fields need to be changed they can be selected singly or by using the mouse + Ctrl can be selected in specific groups.

A graphic can be entered into the form header. Firstly, select the header section – the top line should change colour.

- From the Form Design Tools, Design Ribbon, select the **Insert Image** control. Using the mouse 'draw' a box to the size required, in the header. The system will go to the file directory – from that choose the clip provided (or choose one previously saved in a file – don't use clipart if possible). The graphic will fit itself into the drawn frame.
- To resize the image to fill the frame, select the Format Ribbon on the Form Tools and click on Size/Space ▾ and choose **To fit**. This can also be done more quickly by right-clicking on the graphic and from the pop-up menu – choose the same option.

- To enhance the label in the header, right-click on the label and from the pop-up methods, choose to apply a special effect, background colour and font colour. The whole section colour can be changed – right-click anywhere on the header section and choose a background colour – white is a good option.

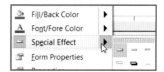

A label and/or graphic can be entered into the form footer. However, it is not immediately available and has to be selected – to do this drag down a space suitable to insert a label. Remember, use the Label *Aa* option from the Controls ▾.

- In the label box, key-in the text as requested – enhance it in the same way as the form header.

The field name objects can also be enhanced – with background colour, font colour and special effects – use the mouse + Ctrl key to select them.

The Details objects can be enhanced – font colour, background colour and special effects. They can also be individually resized to suit the detail that needs to be displayed; for example, a number detail field doesn't need to be as big as a text or memo detail field.

> **Note**
>
> If you copy and paste a graphic it sometimes resizes the header space to a ridiculous size – wasting precious time in an assessment/ assignment situation.

Hints & tips ⭐

For your Higher Assignment/Assessment you will be expected to put your name in the page footer. This is not immediately available either and must be selected – right-click and use the pop-up menu as before.
*Use the Label **Aa** option from the Controls ▾ as before to put your name and centre in the page footer. It won't show on the screen – only on the printout.*

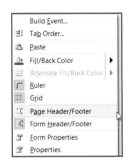

The Finished design could look something like this:

Design View

Form View

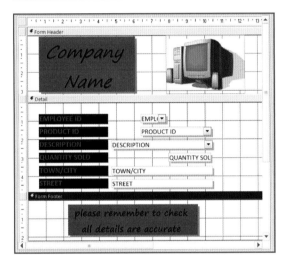

Hints & tips ⭐

*To print a single copy of the form, ensure you select ◎ **Selected Record(s)** from the Print Dialogue Box.*

Print Range	Copies
◎ All	Number of Copies: 1 ▲▼
◎ Pages From: To:	
◉ Selected Record(s)	1¹ 2² 3³ ☐ Collate

Hints & tips ⭐

*Creating Reports is covered in Chapter 4, **National 4&5 Administration and IT**, page 66, Anne Bradley and Adam Stephenson, Hodder Gibson.*

3 Advanced reports

The following advanced skills are required for assessments and the final assignment. Make sure you practise these as much as possible – to make sure you attain the highest marks possible.

Deleting automatic information in a report.

- Select the Text Box to be deleted, it is not a label.

- Delete it using the delete key – not the backspace key – this only deletes the text, not the box and will result in the box displaying "Unbound".

Note !

If this box is used to display a label (for example, text keyed in), it causes the software to ask for Parameter Values!

Reducing field (column) widths

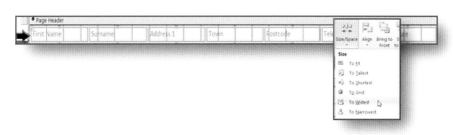

- Select the complete row in the page header section in **Design View**. Clicking the mouse will change it into a black arrow.
- Once selected, right-click and select **To Fit** in the first instance, and then **To Widest**.

Inserting Summary Options

Groupings and **aggregates** can be applied while in the Report Wizard.

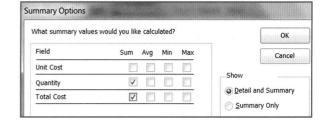

The Grouping Option must be selected before Summary Options can become available – think about it, you can only add or average similar (i.e. grouped by field name) data.

In **Design View** extra labelling can be deleted, edited and any number can be formatted – using the Properties menu (remember right-click to bring up the Options). In fact, the labels look like gobbledegook!! – as can be seen in the excerpt from Design View.

Note !

This wizard automatically generates the aggregates BUT it also generates meaningless labels and extra information.

This can be edited as follows:
- Start by selecting and deleting the unnecessary information which is automatically generated by the wizard *e.g. the summary information in the footer*. Use delete **not** backspace.
- Change **Sum** to something meaningful, for example, **Total Per Category**.
- Change **Avg** to **Average Per Category**.

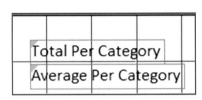

Numbers have to be formatted to make them fit for purpose – i.e. professional. If currency format is required:
- Select the boxes to be formatted (use the Shift key to select more than one).
- Right-click and Select Properties from the pop-up Menu.
- Format for Currency from the Property Sheet.

Numbers may also need to be formatted for decimal places (especially averages which can display quite long decimals).
- Select the boxes to be formatted as before.
- Right-click and select Properties.
- Format for Fixed Number and Zero, one or two decimal places as required.

Count is not available in the Summary Options in the wizard but it is simple to add in **Design View**.
- Select 'Report Footer' section as normal.
- From the **Design** Ribbon, select the **ab|**(Text Box icon) and using the mouse draw the box in the report footer.
- Edit the text in the Text box to – **Number of Something**.
- In the Unbound box key-in: =Count([Field Name]).

e.g.

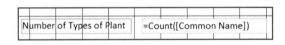

= sign indicates a calculation,
Count is the aggregate function,
(…) specifies a range of data,
[…] denotes the field being counted.

Design View

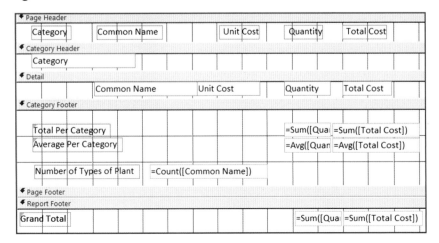

Or

- In Design View, click on the Field in the Detail section and select Count Values from the ∑ Totals as shown.

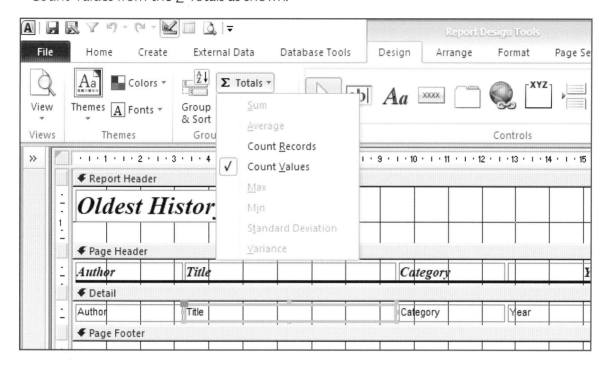

Note: Take care with this as you will have to insert a label using the **Aa** icon to give the count some meaning – e.g. **Number of Books**.

Print Preview

Category	Common Name	Unit Cost	Quantity	Total Cost
Annual				
	Begoniaceae	£12.00	900	£10,800.00
	Blanket Flower	£1.50	500	£750.00
	Coleus	£2.50	370	£925.00
	Fuchsia	£2.00	400	£800.00
	Hibiscus	£2.80	460	£1,288.00
	Petunia	£0.75	1600	£1,200.00
	Sage	£1.20	1750	£2,100.00
	Spider Flower	£3.00	450	£1,350.00
	Verbena	£2.00	1300	£2,600.00
Total Per Category			7730	£21,813.00
Average Per Category			859	£2,423.67
Number of Types of Plant		9		

Ensuring all information is visible

Sometimes Detail Fields contain large amounts of data (which may need to be wrapped?). Remember, the Report Wizard automatically crops data to 'Fit to one page'.

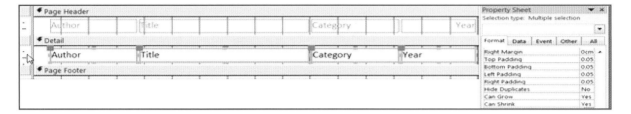

🖰 Select the Detail Row – black arrow denotes this

🖰 Right-click on the selected fields and click on Properties.

🖰 Scroll down the Format options to **Can Grow/Shrink**.

🖰 Change **No** to **Yes** in both boxes.

Author	Title	Category	Year
Ambler, J. Richard	Anasazi, The	United States	1989
Archambeault, James & Thomas D. Clark	Gift Of Pleasant Hill, The	United States	1991
Berton, Pierre	Arctic Grail, The	World	1988
Brown, Craig, Ed.	Illustrated History Of Canada, The	World	1991
Carter, Joseph H.	Nver Met A Man I Didn't Like: The Life And Writings Of Will Rogers	United States	1991

This allows longer detail to be accommodated by extending the field space to suit, while leaving brief detail with the default size – in other words, no lost marks because something is not visible.

Chapter 6

Use of complex functions of word processing to support administrative tasks

What you should know

There is **one** topic to this chapter. By the end of this chapter you should be able to:

1 Edit large documents using advanced functions.

Organisations need to be able to produce business documents to a very high standard. Often, the first impression of an organisation that a customer or supplier or a bank gets is when they receive a printed document.

There are many different documents which need to be produced/edited in the course of performing the many and varied administrative tasks done within an organisation. Most organisations have very particular ideas on how these documents should be laid out, even stipulating the size and type of font required. The reason for this is that most organisations want to ensure a professional and consistent approach to all printed documents. This is called House style.

House style is very important as a uniform style on all documents means that they look more professional by keeping to the same format and style throughout. They are instantly recognisable giving customers and/ or suppliers the ability to recognise at a glance who has sent them that document. If the logo, layout, colour scheme, graphics, etc. changes from one business document to another it looks very careless and unprofessional.

> *Note*
>
> House style refers to an organisation's preferred manner of presentation and layout of printed materials.

The following are examples of the type of documents you will need to be familiar with as to layouts, etc.

- **Letters** – to customers, suppliers, outside agencies, etc.
- **Booklets** – multi-page documents containing information and data in the form of continuous text, tables, contents page, section breaks, references, etc. – usually for use outwith the organisation.
- **Reports** – same as booklets – usually for use within the organisation.
- **Forms** – this could include order forms, application forms, feedback forms, etc. – for use within and outwith the organisation.
- Other documents such as **agendas**, **minutes**, **itineraries** – usually for use within the organisation – also have uniform layouts.

1 Editing large documents using advanced functions

By the end of this section – and with repeated practice – you should be familiar with the advanced functions required to edit large documents.

Advanced functions	
Creating and editing single and multi-page documents, DTP posters, including: • Single and multi-page letters • Booklets • Reports	• Page layout: modified styles, page breaks, section breaks, columns and column breaks, and different page orientation within a document. • Document enhancement: creating front page[1], customised bullets (including symbols)[1], graphics[1], page borders[1], watermarks, etc. • Headers and footers: inserting text, numbers and/or graphics – to specific requirements. • Comments: insert and delete comments. • Referencing: table of contents, footnotes and endnotes, cross referencing, hyperlinks and bookmarks. • Inserting and/or editing text: importing text, keying-in text from written manuscript including manuscript corrections[1] and mail merge[1]. • Altering text: formatting, alignment, line spacing, find and replace. • Booklet layout: including duplex printing[1]. • DTP features for promotional and internal posters, flyers, etc[1].
Creating and editing tables including: • Order forms • Application forms • Itineraries • Agendas • Minutes	• Design functions: table styles (plain and grid style): cell shading and colour, border styles and colours[1]. • Layout/DTP functions: inserting/deleting rows/columns[1], merging and splitting individual cells[1], cell alignment, converting tables to text and vice versa, sorting data and inserting formula to numerical data.

The following task covers many of the advanced functions required for this course, i.e. a multi-page document with contents page, headers and footers, different page orientation, line spacing, referencing, etc.

- Create and save a document – **Large document practice**. (See Appendix 3, page 153, for details on how to create this document.)
- Save the document with a new filename – **Large document edited**.

---

(1) Many of the functions required by the Higher syllabus should be known to you if you have used *National 4 & 5 Administration and IT* when preparing for the National 5 exam. The *National 4 & 5* textbook contains step-by-step instructions for these functions. At Higher level you will have to apply similar functions to documents to a more advanced level and with less guidance.

At the top of the document – place the cursor and insert two section breaks using Page Layout -> Breaks ▼ -> Section Breaks -> Next Page.

✓ Check that your document has two more pages than before (6 pages).

Before editing the document it is important – for the purposes of this document – that the Styles are modified as follows:

🖰 From the Styles section of the Home Ribbon, right-click on Normal and select Modify.

🖰 Change the font to Trebuchet MS size 11.

🖰 Format the paragraph (bottom of dialogue box) to single line spacing (the default is multiple – 1.15) and 0 pt above and 0 pt below.

The whole document will now be this font and single line spacing. It may be necessary to adjust the spacing between paragraphs – do this before proceeding.

🖰 Repeat this procedure for Heading 1 – change font to Trebuchet MS 16, **Bold** and Blue – check the paragraph spacing; it should be 0 pt above and 0 pt below.

🖰 Repeat this procedure for **Heading 2** – change font to Trebuchet MS 14, *Italics* and **Red** – check the paragraph spacing; it should be 0 pt above and 0 pt below.

🖰 Apply Heading 1 formatting to First Section, Second Section, Third Section and Final Section.

🖰 Apply **Heading 2** formatting to the first line of the table (in Third Section) – Weekly Staff Rota.

Go to the first page (*Ctrl Home*) and key-in **Front Page** and increase the font to **72** pt.

Centre this page – both horizontally and vertically – (vertical alignment is on the Page Layout Ribbon Page Setup).

Insert a graphic (from Clip Art). Format the graphic using the Picture Tools, Format Ribbon.

On the Page Layout Ribbon, select the Page Borders icon on the Page Background – make sure you select **This section only** from the **Apply to:** box.

(In Office 2013 this is in the DESIGN Ribbon.)

Creating a contents page

Go to the top of the next (blank) page (page 2). As you have already assigned styles to your paragraph headings, simply select the References Ribbon and from the Table of Contents ▼ section select 'Automatic Table 1'.

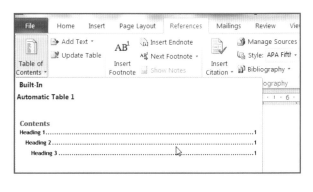

There is no need to key-in the word 'Contents' – the wizard does it automatically.

Don't make any changes to this page (line spacing, font etc.) till you have completed all the edits.

- Because only two styles have been assigned (Heading 1 and Heading 2) the contents pages will only pick up these headings – known as level 1 and level 2.
- When a table of contents is created hyperlinks are also created that link the headings in the table of contents to the headings in your document. To follow the link, just hold the Ctrl key and click on one of the headings in the table of contents to go to that place in the document.

Converting text to table and table to text

Go to the tabulated data in the Second section and select the five rows – make sure you don't select the space above and below these five rows.

From the **Insert** Ribbon ▶ **Table** select the Convert Text to Table option. The dialogue box which appears will automatically calculate that you need a 2 column 5 row table.

(NB If this doesn't happen check that you haven't selected any of the rows above or below the required text.)

- Click OK and the text will now be in the form of a table.
- Adjust the column widths to suit the text and use the AutoFit Contents option on the Table Tools ▶ Layout Ribbon.
- Go to the table below the next paragraph and select the table.

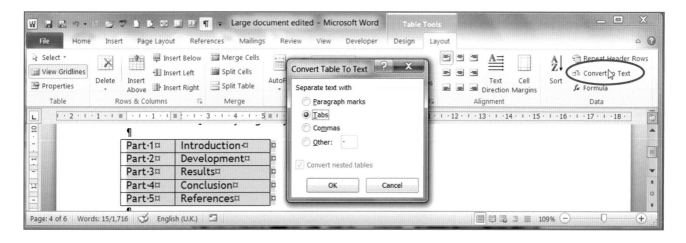

- From the Table Tools ▶ Layout Ribbon select Convert to Text.
- The pop-up dialogue box will automatically select Tabs – which is exactly what is required. Click OK.

Changing the layout of one page within a large document

- Place the cursor immediately above the table – Weekly Staff Rota.
- From the Page Layout Ribbon, select Breaks ▶ Section Break ▶ Next Page.
- Place the cursor immediately after the table and repeat Step 2.

Place the cursor back above the table again and from the Page Layout Ribbon ▶ Orientation ▶ select Landscape. This page, and only this page, will be formatted as landscape and the rest of the document will be formatted as portrait.

Changing the line spacing of the main body text

- Place the cursor in front of the heading First Section.
- To select the body of the text, press *Shift+Ctrl+End* (i.e. not front page and not contents page).

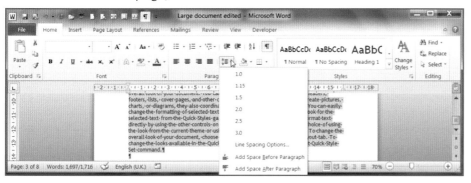

- Select 1.5 line spacing from the Home Ribbon ▶ Paragraph line spacing icon. The body of the text is now in 1.5 line spacing (front page and contents page unchanged).

Changing one paragraph from single column to a three column format

- Select the paragraph before the **Final Section** (remember triple-click within the paragraph or double-click with the cursor arrow at the left-hand side of the document).

- From the Page Layout Ribbon ▶ Columns, select option Three. This will automatically insert a ===Section Break (Continuous)=== above and below the paragraph which allows you to change line spacing and columns without having to do anything. Your text in this paragraph should be in three columns – this is DTP feature of Word Processing.

- If you need to edit the size of the columns, insert a Page Break ▶ Column – the text following will be moved to the next column.

Inserting a footnote and an endnote

Place the cursor at the end of the Heading **Second Section** and from the References Ribbon ▶ select Insert Footnote from the Footnotes section. The cursor will appear at the very bottom of the page with a continuous line above it and a small number 1.

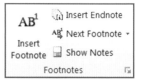

- Key-in – This is an example of a footnote – the font will be smaller than the rest of the text.
- To return to your place in the text – double-click on the small number of the footnote.
- Hover the mouse over the small number above the text and the contents of the footnote will be displayed.

The process is the same for endnotes. Place the cursor at the end of the Heading **Third Section** and from the References Ribbon ▶ select Insert Endnote from the Footnotes section. The cursor will appear at the very end of the document with a continuous line above it and a small number i.

Key-in – This is an example of an endnote – the font will also be smaller than the rest of the text.

Note !

Footnotes and endnotes are automatically re-numbered as you move text around a document, insert another note or delete a note. By accessing the arrow on the bottom right-hand corner, you can change the number format and even replace the numbers with symbols.

When deleting a footnote NEVER delete the text – simply go to the reference number within the text, select it and then delete the reference – the note will be deleted.

(If you delete the text you will be left with the continuous line and the reference number within the body of the text!)

Enhancing the table on landscape page

At Higher level, it is expected that a table should be resized to fill the landscape space.

Resize the table (by placing the mouse on the bottom right-hand corner and drag diagonally to fill the whole page) – make sure you have view set at one-page.

- Select the whole table and increase the font size to 18 pt.
- Using the Table Tools Design Ribbon – Apply simple gridlines.
- Using the Table Tools Layout Ribbon – Merge the top row.
- Fill (shade) with a colour.
- Centre the Column and Row Headings (use the same colour).
- Check that the heading – **Weekly Staff Rota** – still has the **Heading 2** style assigned (otherwise it will disappear from the contents page).

Inserting headers and footers

At Higher level it is expected that your name is on every printout and, unless otherwise instructed, it is a good idea to do this in the header as quite often the assignment has specific/complicated instructions for the footer.

- Go to the top of your document (remember Ctrl + Home) and from the Insert Ribbon choose Header ▶ Edit Header.
- The cursor should be in Header Section 1.

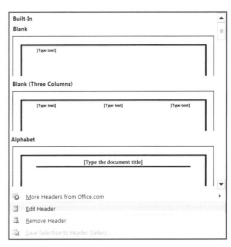

The **Header & Footer Tools** Design Ribbon should be activated and visible at the top of the document.

- Check the Different Odd & Even Pages from the Options section of the Ribbon.
- Key-in – Prepared by Your Name – the font can be reduced, aligned left, centre or right. For this document **Centre** this text and reduce to Font **9**pt.
- In the Navigation section select ▶ Next and the cursor will be taken to **Even Page Header Section 2**.
- De-select the **Link to previous** – it is ESSENTIAL that you do this before keying in anything. Repeat the keying-in as before. Every page should now have your name in the header. (*In business the title of the report, booklet or whatever would appear here.*)

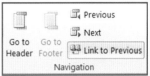

From this Ribbon select **Go to Footer** – try to resist the temptation to scroll down in any of the following instructions – use the functions.

The cursor should now be in the

Even Page Footer – Section 2.

Remember at Higher level, it is expected that you know that the contents page is NOT numbered.

- Select ▶ Next again and the cursor will now be in

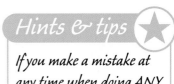

Hints & tips

*If you make a mistake at any time when doing ANY edits simply press **Undo** (Ctrl + Z) – don't try to fix it – it usually just gets WORSE!!!!*

Odd Page Footer – Section 3   Same as Previous.

- 🖱 De-select the **Link to previous** – AGAIN!
- 🖱 From the Header & Footer section of this Ribbon select Page Number ▾ Current Position, Plain Number.
- 🖱 Perhaps you could enhance this footer with a line above the text. The default number will be **3** as it is page **3** of the document; however, the body of the text should read page **1**. Follow the first step to select the Page Number Format dialogue box, and edit the Start at box to begin at **1** > OK.
- 🖱 Insert a graphic (the same as on the front page?) on the right-hand side of the footer – make it very small and format it to Wrap Behind Text.
- 🖱 Select ▶ Next again and the cursor will now be in

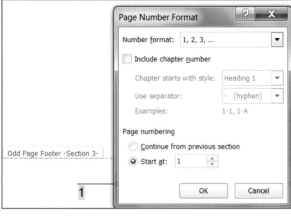

Even Page Footer – Section 3   Same as Previous.

- 🖱 De-select the **Link to previous** – yes AGAIN! Press the tab key twice to get to the right-hand side of the document and follow the same procedure to enter the next page number, insert the same graphic on the left-hand side of the footer and of course the line above the text.

    Select ▶ Next again and the cursor will now be in

At Higher grade, it is expected that the footer be edited so that anything on the right-hand side should be aligned right. In this case it is a graphic but sometimes it can be specific text. It is important that **all** instructions are followed.

- 🖱 De-select the **Link to previous** and grab the graphic with the mouse and place right over to the right-hand side of the footer.
- 🖱 Select ▶ Next AGAIN and the cursor will now be in

    Even Page Footer – Section 5   Same as Previous.

Congratulations!

If you have followed the instructions carefully, you should have eight pages in your document – front page, contents page and six numbered pages of text.

Updating a contents page

The simplest way to get to the required page is to use the **G**o **T**o Function (Ctrl + G).

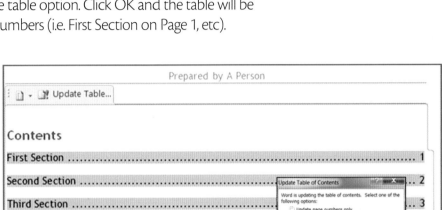

- Key-in **2** in the Enter page number: box and click on **Go To** and **Close**.
- Click anywhere in the Contents section and the whole object will be selected. Click on Update Table and select Update entire table option. Click OK and the table will be updated to show new page numbers (i.e. First Section on Page 1, etc).

- Go To First Section heading and change to – Introduction.
- Go To Final Section heading and change to – Conclusion.
- Go To page two and simply click on the **Update Table** and the new headings will appear – like magic!
- Select the main text in the **Contents** object and change to double (2) line spacing.

Your final document should look something like this.

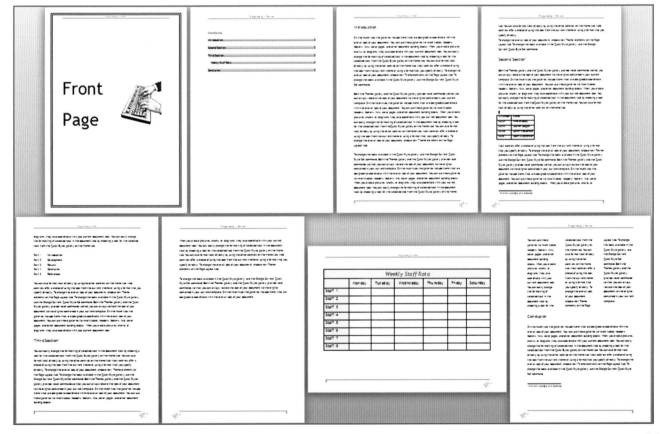

🖱 Save and close the document.

You can practise this MANY times so that editing multi-page documents becomes second nature – just remember to save it with a different name every time. Do it no less than five times to make sure you are an **EXPERT!**

Bookmarks, cross-references and hyperlinks

🖱 Open **Large document edited** (the first one if you have more than one). Select the tab section (Section 2, page 5) and select Bookmark from the Insert Ribbon. (*In Office 2013 this is hidden below Links ▾ on the Insert Ribbon.*)

🖱 In the pop-up dialogue box, key-in an appropriate name – in this case key-in – Programme.

🖱 Go to the three-column section (Section 3, page 8). Select Bookmark as before and key-in – Columns (i.e. overtype the previous word). Click Add.

🖱 Check that you have done this by using Ctrl + Home and Go To function.

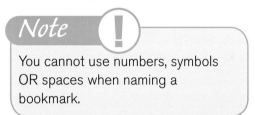

Note !

You cannot use numbers, symbols OR spaces when naming a bookmark.

Creating a cross-reference

A cross-reference allows you to link to other parts of the same document. You might use a cross-reference to link to a chart or graphic that appears elsewhere in the document. The cross-reference appears as a link that takes the reader to the referenced item. To allow users to jump to the referenced item, select the Insert as a hyperlink check box. When you insert the cross-reference, you'll see a dialogue box that lists everything that's available to link to. If you want to link to a separate document you can create a hyperlink.

Note !

A hyperlink is a link from a document to a place in another location, activated by clicking on a highlighted word or image. Bookmarks, etc. are hyperlinks.

Creating a hyperlink

By simply keying in a website address, the software automatically creates a hyperlink.

🖱 Use the **Large document edited**.

🖱 Save As **Large document edited 2**.

🖱 Place the cursor at the end of the first paragraph key-in – www.hoddereducation.co.uk – as soon as you press the space bar, the text will immediately change colour and be underlined – making it a hyperlink.

If required, it is easy to remove the hyperlink by right-clicking on the web address and selecting the option X Remove Hyperlink.

Creating a hyperlink using a graphic

🖱 Select the graphic (on the Front Page).

🖱 Right-click on the graphic and select Insert Hyperlink in the pop-up dialogue box. Key-in the same address (in the Address box ▼) as before and click OK.

You can also create a hyperlink to another document by following the steps on the Insert Hyperlink dialogue box. For example, you can do this by selecting one of the Link to: options on the left-hand side of the box.

Using review functions on the Review Ribbon

Adding comments

When you want to add notes, suggestions or questions to a document but don't want to change the actual content, you can insert comments – they are easily added as follows:

🖱 Select the text or item you want to comment on.

🖱 From the Review Ribbon, select New Comment.

🖱 Type the comment/suggestion/question in the comment Balloon.

When you are finished with the comments you can delete them easily.

🖱 Use the Large document edited 2.

🖱 Place the cursor at the end of the second paragraph.

🖱 From the Review Ribbon select New Comment and key-in the following text.

> This is an example of a comment. It can be deleted by right-clicking and using the pop-up menu **OR** selecting Delete from the comments section of the Review Ribbon.

Comments are automatically numbered. The balloon will also show information about the system, the time and date created, etc.

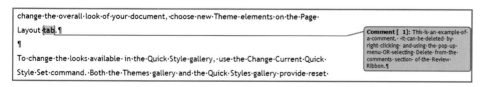

Using word count

To see the word count in your document, look at the status bar at the bottom left-hand side of the Word window. It will show the number of pages, which page you are on and the number of words.

However, if you need or want more information, choose Word Count from the Proofing Section (left-hand side) of the Review Ribbon.

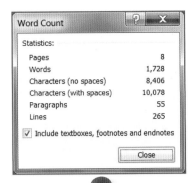

Applying a watermark

Watermarks are text or pictures placed **behind** the document text. They can mark the document's status as Draft, Confidential, etc., brand it with a logo, or just make it look better.

- Still using the **Large document edited 2**.
- From the Page Layout Ribbon select **Watermark ▾**.
- Select Custom Watermark from the pop-down menu and select the ◎ Text watermark option on the dialogue box.
- Place the cursor in the Text: area and key-in Practice task (this will overwrite the suggested texts), change the font and colour (choose as shown or decide for yourself). Click OK.

The finished document should look something like this:

Remember

Use the Undo (Formatting) function (CTRL + Z) if you get too mixed up.

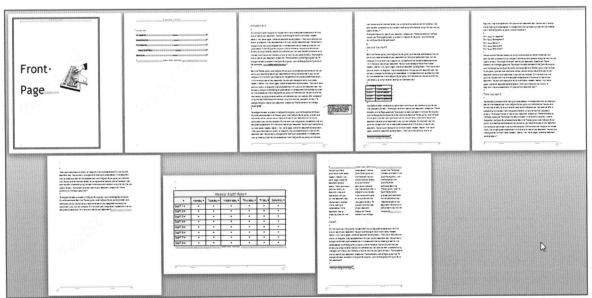

Creating a form for electronic completion

Before beginning to make a form, check that the Ribbons include the Developer Ribbon. If no such Ribbon is there, select **Customize Ribbon** from the **File ▶ Options** menu. Check the box beside Developer. The Developer Ribbon will now be at the right-hand side of the Ribbons. The tools needed to make an electronic form are in the Controls section. The controls from previous versions of Word are accessed by clicking on the ▾ arrow.

An interactive form is a document that has instructions with questions and spaces reserved for answers. A space reserved for an answer is called a form field. You can create fields in which users can type their responses in text boxes.

A text form field can be formatted to contain alphabetic, numeric, dates, times, etc. You can also create a list of choices by using a Drop-down field[2] or a set of Check boxes[3]. Forms can be printed out so that users can respond on paper but they are specially tailored so that a form can be filled out using a computer. Word allows you to protect the form so that users can make their entries and selections, BUT THEY CANNOT ALTER THE LAYOUT OF THE FORM. You can create many types of interactive forms – application forms, invoices, time sheets, order forms, etc. – these can be uploaded onto intranets and internet websites.

Note

Form field: A location in a form where users can respond to a question OR specify an appropriate response.
Drop-down field: A field that allows users to display a list of choices and select a response.
Check Boxes: A field that allows users to choose from multiple options by clicking a box.

After completing this task you will be able to:

✔ Add text form fields and set the field properties.
✔ Add drop-down form fields and set the field properties.
✔ Add check box form fields and set the field properties.
✔ Edit the form and Protect the form.
✔ Complete a form – *on computer*.

The **form** will have specific questions and pre-prepared answers, space for individual information (*formatted to reduce keyboarding errors*), an automatic date field and check boxes for indicating choice.

🖱 Open the file named **Option form – table**, to convert into an interactive form
🖱 Save As – **Interactive Option Form**. Do this immediately.

Hints & tips ⭐

Remember to select the show/hide icon ¶ - this will help you to see all formatting easily.

_____

(2) A field that allows users to display a list of choices and select a response.
(3) A field that allows users to click a box to choose from multiple options.

We are now ready to edit the table to become a form. It is a good idea to click on the Show/Hide button on the toolbar to make formatting, etc. easier.

 Position the cursor in the space (cell) for **Surname**.

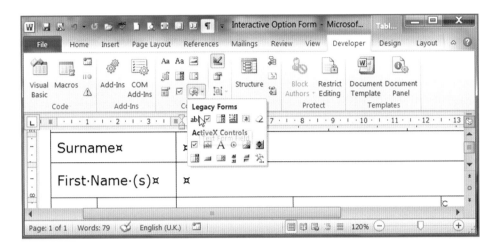

 Click on the 'Text form field' button – ONCE ONLY. A field will appear – ooooo – double-click on this and a dialogue box will appear. This allows the formatting of the field to be refined. In this case:

- Select Regular Text (the default).
- Change the length to 50 (this will save a lot of text being entered wrongly into a box and therefore distorting the shape of your form).
- Key-in to Default Text, '**Enter Your Surname**'.
- Select Title Case in Text format (so that the Surname always appears with an initial capital).
- Click OK.

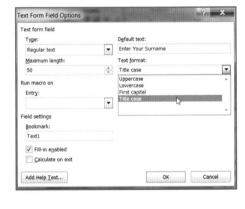

 Complete the **First Name(s)** box in the same way.

Note !

You could also format the rest of the form in the same way but to ensure accuracy and the least amount of keying-in for the user of the form it is better to use drop-down menus and a combination of check boxes.

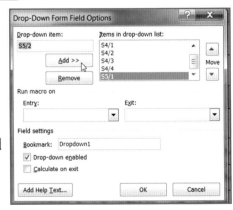

 Position the Cursor in the cell to the right of Class and click on the Drop-Down Form Field (*from the Legacy Forms*). Again double-click on the shaded area which appears and a dialogue box will appear. So that a blank space will show on the form press the space bar once and click ADD>>.

 Enter 4/1 and ADD>>. Proceed in this manner until you have entered all the possible classes (in this case classes 4/1 – 4/4 and 5/1 – 5/2). Click OK.

🖱 Position the Cursor in the cell to the right of Date – to format a date field which will always default to the current date. Follow the procedure for Text Form Field and format the options:

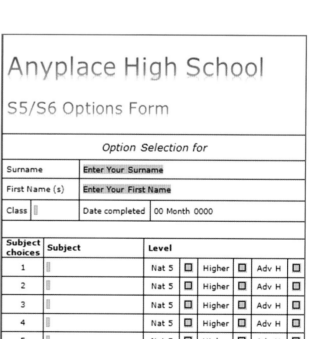

🖱 Type – Current date

🖱 Date format – dd MMMM yyyy

🖱 Position the cursor in the first cell below Subject and select the Drop-down button from the toolbar. Enter two subjects – **English** and **Mathematics** remembering to insert a blank space at the top as we did for the Class.

In Subject 2 cell, simply copy and paste this field (or do it again yourself if you feel you need the practice).

- For Subject 3 follow the same procedure as before but enter the subjects as follows.

Biology, History, Geography, Modern Studies and Business Management.

The order can be easily changed by selecting Move with the arrow buttons to the right of the list.

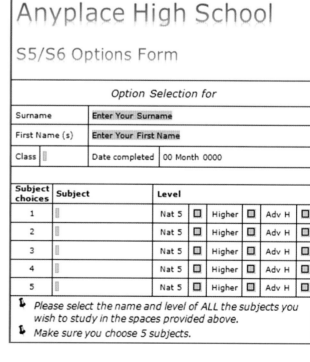

🖱 Follow the same procedure for Subject 4 and enter the details as follows.

Administration, Chemistry, Graphic Communication, Art and French.

Rearrange the list in alphabetical order by selecting and Moving with the arrow buttons.

🖱 Complete Subject 5 with the details as follows.

Accounting, Business Management, German, Music, PE, Physics, RME and Spanish.

🖱 In the first space for Level, click the Check-box[4] once and double-click on the box to refine the formatting. For example, you may want to make the check boxes smaller. Complete the rest of the spaces by clicking the check box (use your down arrow key to speed up the process).

Your form should hopefully look something like this:

Modifying and protecting form fields

You can modify a form just as you modify any document. You can add a page border, text formatting, add graphics, more cells to the table, etc. You can also modify the form FIELDS within a form. You can add frames or borders to form fields, remove the default shading for each field and you can specify new options (called Properties) in the form field options dialogue boxes.

Anyplace High School

S5/S6 Options Form

Option Selection for						
Surname	Enter Your Surname					
First Name (s)	Enter Your First Name					
Class ▯		Date completed	00 Month 0000			

Subject choices	Subject	Level					
1	▯	Nat 5	☐	Higher	☐	Adv H	☐
2	▯	Nat 5	☐	Higher	☐	Adv H	☐
3	▯	Nat 5	☐	Higher	☐	Adv H	☐
4	▯	Nat 5	☐	Higher	☐	Adv H	☐
5	▯	Nat 5	☐	Higher	☐	Adv H	☐

↳ *Please select the name and level of ALL the subjects you wish to study in the spaces provided above.*
↳ *Make sure you choose 5 subjects.*

---

(4) A field that allows users to select an option by clicking the appropriate box.

Once you have modified all the fields and you are satisfied that the form is complete, you MUST **protect it** (Restrict Editing) as follows:

- 🖰 Click on the Restrict Editing on the Developer Ribbon ▾ Protect section.
- 🖰 On the Restrict Formatting and Editing▾, select 2 – Editing restrictions
- 🖰 **Allow only this type of editing in the document:** Select **Filling in** Forms from the ▾ pull down list.
- 🖰 Select 3 – **Yes, Start Enforcing Protection**.
- 🖰 You will be prompted to apply a password.

The form is now interactive and can be completed electronically as follows.

Remember

You can just as easily unprotect the form (allow editing) if you discover errors in your design or changes in data or whatever.

However, responses cannot be entered into a form until Restrict Editing has been applied.

Activity

1 Name of Student – Mary Mackay class 4/4.
2 Save As – M Mackay-options.
3 Select subject choices as follows:

English Higher, Maths Nat 5, Business Management Higher, Administration and IT Higher, Spanish Nat 5.

4 Save again before closing.

As an extra task:

5 Email BOTH forms to your teacher for evidence.

Saving a form as a template

You can also save a form as a template (different to a document) which is also password protected so that it cannot be altered by unathorised users – you would select Word Template from the bottom of the Save As screen – *however, do not do this for this task.*

Glossary of terms for forms

Terminology	Meaning
Check box form field	A field that allows the users to select an option by clicking a check box with the mouse (or pressing the space bar).
Default	A choice made by a program when the user does not specify an alternative answer or option.
Drop-down form field	A field that allows users to display a list of descriptive choices from which they can select a response.
Form	A document with instructions, questions and fields reserved for users to enter responses.
Form field	A location in a form where users can respond to a question or specify an appropriate response.

Terminology	Meaning
Properties	The ability to change the way a form field behaves and accepts entries (such as date format in a text form field) or, for a list form field, the ability to change the entries that appear in the list.
Text form field	On a form, a box in which users can type a text response to a question or instruction. Depending on the format specified for a text form field, the field can contain alphnumeric characters, numbers only, dates or times.

Field options	Refers to:
Regular Text	A field that can contain any type of characters, including numbers, symbols and letters. You specify a default entry to appear in the form by typing it in the Default Text box in the Text Form Field Options dialogue box.
Number	A field that requires a numeric entry. You specify a default entry to appear in the form by typing it in the Default Number Box in the Text Form Field Options dialogue box.
Date	A field that requires a date entry. Users can enter the date in any valid date format – 8 October 2017, 08/10/17, 8 Oct 17, etc. The date users enter will be converted to the date format that is specified in the Text Form Field Options dialogue box.
Current date	A field that always displays the current date. Word supplies this field when the form is opened, and the current date is inserted using the date format that you specify.
Current time	As for date, and current date.
Calculation	A field that contains a formula you can use to enter a calculation, such as a calculation to display a total order amount by multiplying a price by quantity ordered – useful for order forms, invoices etc.

Adding formulae to a table

🖱 Create a simple table as follows:

Day	Takings (£)
Monday	300.50
Tuesday	295.00
Wednesday	400.60
Thursday	500.40
Friday	550.00
Total	

🖱 On the bottom right-hand cell select the ***fx*** formula symbol on the Table Tools Layout Ribbon.

🖱 The pop-up dialogue box will show the default (=SUM(**ABOVE**)).

🖱 Select the currency option from the Number format.

🖱 Click OK – the last row of the table should now contain the Total = £2,056.50.

Now try the formula for AVERAGE:

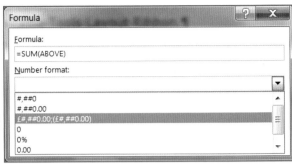

- 🖱 In the bottom left-hand cell, delete the word Total and replace with Average.
- 🖱 Delete the formula for Total and select the **fx** formula again.
- 🖱 Overwrite SUM and key in AVERAGE (=AVERAGE (ABOVE)) and choose the currency option.
- 🖱 Click OK – the last row of the table should now contain Average = £409.30.

Now try the formula for MINIMUM:

- 🖱 As before, delete the word Average and replace with Minimum Takings.
- 🖱 Delete the formula for Average and select the **fx** formula again.
- 🖱 Overwrite AVERAGE and key-in MIN (=MIN(ABOVE)) and choose the currency option.
- 🖱 Click OK – the last row of the table should now contain Minimum Takings = £295.00.

Now try the formula for MAXIMUM:

- 🖱 As before, delete the words Minimum Takings and replace with Maximum Takings.
- 🖱 Delete the formula for Minimum and select the **fx** formula again.
- 🖱 Overwrite MIN and key in MAX (=MAX(ABOVE)) and choose currency option.
- 🖱 Click OK – the last row of the table should now contain Maximum Takings = £550.00.

Integrating data from other IT applications dynamically

To do this:

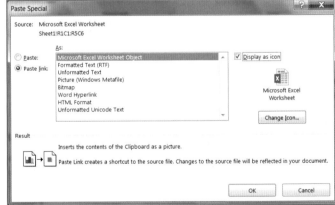

- 🖱 Copy the data – most commonly a spreadsheet table or a chart.
- 🖱 Paste into the document using Paste Special from the drop-down **Paste ▾ menu.**
- 🖱 Select – ◎ Paste link – creating a link to the source file – and any changes in the source file will be changed in the document – in other words, the pasted data are dynamically linked.

Note !

You need to practise, practise, practise these advanced skills until they become second nature. Your assessments and final assignment will not come with such detailed instructions – in fact, you will have to problem solve! So it makes sense to make sure you can perform all of the advanced functions required by the course without having to think too much – if you are expert you will save time which is limited in the Assessments and Final Assignment.

Chapter 7

Communicating complex information to a range of audiences using IT

What you should know

There are **two** topics covered in this chapter. By the end you should be able to:

1 Create/edit presentation software to communicate information to specific audiences.

2 Use email and e-diary applications to communicate information.

1 Create/edit presentation software to communicate information to specific audiences

Making use of presentation software is a popular method to complement what the speaker is saying. PowerPoint® is one of the most commonly used applications, although Prezi (a cloud-based presentation application) and Keynote (Apple's presentation application) are increasingly popular. Here are some advanced functions of PowerPoint that presenters may choose to use to help them deliver a successful presentation:

Customised/timed animation

Animations are how items within each slide appear; automatically, or with a click of the mouse.

Hints & tips

Functions of PowerPoint such as transitions, animations, sounds, action buttons and printing for assessment purposes should be known to you already. However, the **National 4 & 5 Administration and IT** *textbook contains step-by-step instructions for these functions — which you may need to apply at a more advanced level and with less guidance.*

- Select the object you want to animate.
- From the Animations Ribbon, select a suitable effect.
- From the timing section, there will be a drop-down menu, which will automatically be set to On Click. You can decide to keep it on click, this allows the presenter to decide when to bring objects onto the screen. Alternatively, With Previous will mean the object will appear when the previous object has appeared or After Previous, which will wait until the last item you animated has appeared then it will bring this one on next.
- You are also able to time how long to wait before your object appears after the previous object by entering a suitable time into Delay.

Looped

It is possible to make your presentation continue to show on a loop. This is probably most useful where your presentation is being used to display information on a screen in a reception area. This means once the presentation gets to the last slide, it will just go back to the beginning and start again.

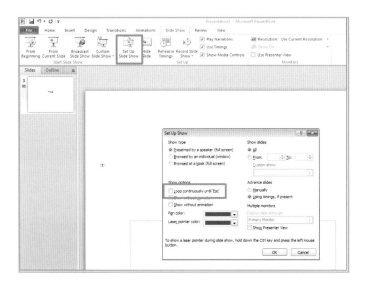

● From the Slide Show Ribbon, select Set Up Slide Show.
● From the Show options section, select Loop continuously until 'Esc'.

Notes

As discussed earlier research, planning and practice are essential for a presentation to be successful. A speaker will often have notes with them to help them navigate their way through their presentation – this will help jog their memory while talking. PowerPoint provides the facility to add any notes that will be used during the presentation to the relevant slide.

● The notes section will automatically show at the bottom of each slide and you are able to add information that will be helpful to the speaker when they are presented.
● The notes are not visible when the presentation is being run.
● The speaker can print the notes out along with the slide to have with them when presenting.

Advance slides automatically

It is possible to time the presentation so that a slide will move on to the next one automatically, without the presenter needing to click manually. It is more likely that this will need to be done when a presentation is running on its own on a screen with information. The danger of using this function when a presenter is speaking is that if they overrun when speaking the slide will move on when they are not ready.

- From the Transitions Ribbon, click After in the Timing section and enter the amount of time that you want the slide to stay on the screen before it moves to the next one.

Advance slides automatically timed to speaker

When rehearsing the presentation, it is possible to run the slide show and PowerPoint will record when you click the mouse to bring in objects and move on to new slides. The timings will then be applied to the presentation for future. This is a useful tool when a presentation will be displayed on screen and needs to move automatically from slide to slide. It can also be used when someone is speaking, but as mentioned before, the danger is the slide may move on when you haven't finished talking about the topic.

- From the Slide Show Ribbon, select Rehearse Timings.
- The slide show begins and you should work through the presentation while practising your speech.
- When the slide show is over you will be asked to confirm that you want to keep the timings.

- If you decide you want to practise again because you didn't get it quite right, you can just click Rehearse Timings again and the new times will be kept, discarding the previous times you had.

Print layout

There are many different print layouts that can be produced from PowerPoint which can be used to help the speaker or audience.

- File > Print
- From the settings section choose the drop-down menu, which will have Full Page Slides already selected, and you will be presented with a range of different print layouts.

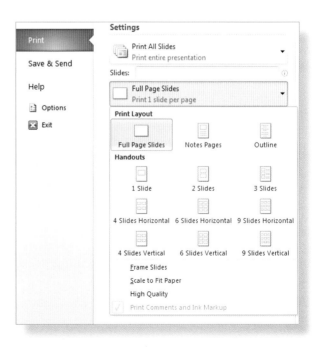

Most of the layouts are self-explanatory, and you can preview what they will look like before sending them to the printer, but here's an explanation of a couple that you might choose to use in different situations:

Notes page – this is the printout that you will want to print for the speaker. It will give them a copy of the slide and then underneath will print any notes that were added to the notes section. This will mean the presenter can see what slide is on the screen and also has some prompts to help them during their speech.

Three slides – this is a useful print layout to issue to the audience. It gives them a copy of the slide show but also leaves some lines for them to make their own notes of what the presenter has said. This saves them having to copy down the slides and they can focus on what is being said.

Remember

Check that your graphics and the text are not covering any information or parts of the slide – this includes the design feature of the slide template.

2 Use email and e-diary applications to communicate information

Email

There are several useful features which can help improve communication.

- **Signature:** contact details of the sender can be set up to appear automatically on all messages – particularly useful for external email messages.
- **Out of Office reply:** this can be set up to reply automatically (with a short message) to the sender, advising them who to contact, etc.
- **Follow-Up Flag/ High Importance:** messages can be marked urgent to encourage the recipient to deal with the matter or a flag can be attached to remind the sender when a reply has not been received.
- **Attachments:** any electronic file (document or spreadsheet or graphic), business card or calendar event can be included in an email.
- **Group emails:** this is done by creating the group in the contacts list for future use.

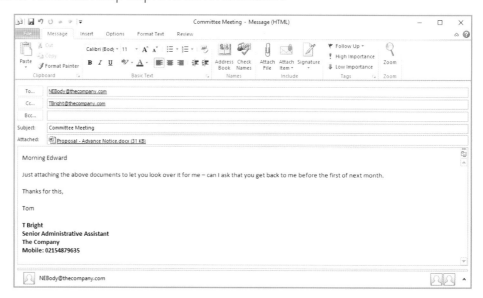

E-diary

The e-diary has a number of features with which you should be familiar and which are useful for supporting the planning and management of events. There are many different providers of e-diary software, but they all tend to have similar features:

- **Title** – this is usually the first text box you are presented with. Here you should enter a brief, clear and simple description of the event or meeting. Remember that you may be sharing the appointment with another person or group who may not be familiar with what is being planned.

- **Location** – here you can enter where the meeting is taking place. This may be a room number or name, for an internal meeting, or an address of a hotel or venue if the meeting is taking place externally.

- **Start/end times** – here you can select a date and time for the meeting to start and finish. A drop-down menu will be provided. In the time section, if the exact time you want is not listed, you can type in a time to overwrite the list. Some appointments may not have a specific time, especially if you are using the diary to remind you to do something, such as update the minutes for a meeting. Clicking 'All day' allows you to pick a date and not a time.

- **Reminders** – a useful feature of the diary is the ability to schedule a reminder. From the drop-down menu you can select when you want to receive the alert, for example, 15 minutes before, a day before. This will usually display a pop-up on your screen which you can dismiss or snooze if you need another reminder later. There is also the option to ask for a reminder to be emailed, which you can request to be sent at a certain day and time and with which you can include a message.

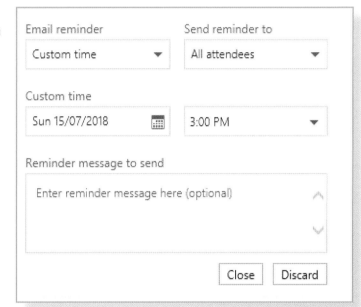

- **Repeat** – a drop-down menu of options is provided with common frequencies (daily, weekly, monthly) but there is also the option of customising the frequency.

- **Attachments** – as with an email, clicking **Attach** enables you to add any file you choose to the appointment. This is useful for previous minutes or an agenda and can avoid the need for a separate email. Any file type can be attached.

- **Notes** – there is a space to add additional notes or comments in a text box. This can be used for a list of things that need to be done for an event or to give more details of what will happen at the event to the participants.

🖱 **Scheduling** – when organising an event for a number of people to attend it can be difficult to find a suitable time for everyone. Most e-dairies have a scheduling function to help with this. Add the addresses of all participants to the meeting and the software will search for the most suitable date and time for the event to take place.

🖱 **Invitations** – adding participants to the appointment entry will send a notification to everyone you have invited to the event. Users can then Accept, Decline or suggest another date/time. Changes made to the appointment entry will automatically update in other users' calendars. You can then also track who is able and not able to attend.

🖱 **Printing** – there will be a facility to print extracts of your e-diary. Do not use the File > Print option as this will print your browser view rather than the diary view. Instead use the Print icon on the web page. This will then allow you to choose the view – day, working week, full week, month or year.

The various features of the e-diary can be seen on the example below.

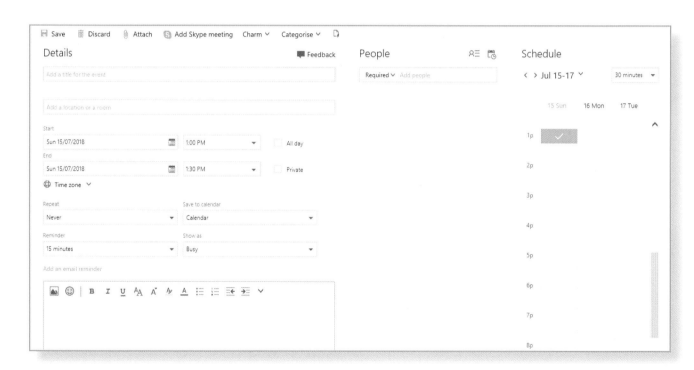

Suggested solutions to exam-style written questions

Chapter 1 Factors contributing to the effectiveness of the administrative practices within an organisation

1 Compare the duties of the Administrative Assistant with those of the Senior Administrative Assistant. (3 marks)

> This question is testing your knowledge AND understanding of the duties of both levels of Administrative Assistants. Your answer should include three of the items below as there is one mark allocated per comparison or similarity.

Remember

The question is asking you to compare the duties of the Senior Administrative Assistant AND the Administrative Assistant including similarities – i.e. duties that THEY BOTH CARRY OUT.

✓ The Senior Administrative Assistant does the type of work more concentrated on the needs of managers **whereas** the Administrative Assistant carries out routine tasks delegated by the Senior Administrative Assistant.

✓ The Senior Administrative Assistant manages the daily schedule of managers and setting up appointments **whereas** the Administrative Assistant deals with incoming calls and greeting and directing visitors with appointments.

✓ The Senior Administrative Assistant prepares reports and presentations for managers to use at meetings **whereas** the Administrative Assistant carries out the copying and emailing of routine documentation as delegated by the Senior Administrative Assistant.

✓ **Both** work with office software and hardware to complete clerical duties such as updating databases, preparing documentation for meetings, updating the e-diary, sending emails with notifications of meetings and ensuring files are managed effectively.

2 Outline four methods which a Senior Administrative Assistant could use to monitor an employee's work. (4 marks)

> This question is testing your knowledge AND understanding of monitoring the quality of time and task management. Your answer should make reference to four of the items below as there is one mark allocated per outline.

Remember

The command word Outline does not require a detailed description.

✓ Check at regular intervals that work is progressing as expected.

✓ Set regular meetings with an employee.

✓ Request regular updates from an employee.

✓ Check progress against Action Plans.

✓ Use a Buddy system where an employee is paired with someone with more experience for help and advice.

✓ Review targets set in an employee's Personal Development Plan.

✓ Use a Gantt chart to compare planned and actual progress/identify if tasks are on track.

✓ Use an appraisal system to discuss progress towards targets.

3 Describe three time management strategies a Senior Administrative Assistant could use to be more effective in the workplace. (6 marks)

> This question is testing your knowledge AND understanding of time and task management strategies. Your answer should make reference to three of the items below as there is one mark allocated per relevant fact and another mark for a further related fact or example. This is illustrated by the use of the dash.

Remember

The command word Describe requires more detail. This can be a mixture of relevant facts and examples relating to the question.

✓ Use To-do Lists of tasks to be done – *updated at the beginning of the day or the end of the day for the next day – arranged in order of importance – to ensure that urgent tasks are completed on time – to allow tasks to be ticked off as/when completed.*

✓ Prepare an Action Plan which breaks down a task into smaller more attainable parts – *to arrange tasks in order of completion – estimate/ decide time for completion/deadline, for example, organising an event.*

✓ Delegate routine tasks to other members of staff – *allows an employee more time to focus on key/urgent tasks.*

✓ Use a Gantt chart to keep tasks on track – *monitor timing of a project using a dateline – implement corrective action if needed by changed priorities.*

✓ Use a proper file management system (both electronic and manual) – *give documents/files appropriate names to assist in easy retrieval – keep an organised desk/desktop.*

4 Justify the need for a Senior Administrative Assistant to monitor and evaluate a Junior Administrative Assistant's work. (3 marks)

> This question is testing your understanding of the importance of effective time and task management. Your answer should make reference to three of the items below as there is one mark allocated per justification.

Remember

This question is asking you to justify something, so think about it and be convincing.

✓ Ensuring that tasks are completed on time.

✓ Ensuring the quality of work being completed.

✓ To review the progress of a task/find out if assistance or resources are needed for a task.

✓ To review and adjust targets for future tasks.

✓ To keep staff on track/ensure staff stay on task and are not distracted.

✓ To help award performance-related pay.

✓ To assist with the staff appraisal process.

✓ To identify future training needs of staff/employees.

5 Outline the reasons why a Senior Administrative Assistant may be reluctant to delegate a task. (2 marks)

> This question is testing your understanding of (reasons why) the importance of delegation to ensure effective time and task management.
>
> Your answer should make reference to two of the items below as there is one mark allocated per outline.

✓ Inability to trust colleagues to complete the work on time.

✓ Fear of loss of status/job security.

✓ Worry that work will be of poor quality.

✓ Fear of upsetting staff/overburdening staff.

✓ Fear of losing control over the task.

6 Describe the long-term implications for a Senior Administrative Assistant who fails to delegate tasks to a Junior Administrative Assistant. (6 marks)

> This question is testing your knowledge AND understanding of the importance of delegation and the implications of failure to delegate. Your answer should make reference to at least two of the items below as there is one mark allocated per relevant fact and additional marks for further related facts or examples. This is illustrated by the use of the dash.

Hints & tips ⭐

Points can be made in any order, for example, fact leading to the implication OR implication caused by a fact!

✓ (Senior Administrative Assistant) may suffer from stress as a result of a heavy workload – could result in employee taking time off through illness – leading to an inability to focus on effective completion of the task.

✓ (Senior Administrative Assistant) may find it difficult to meet deadlines – resulting in lower productivity.

✓ Deadlines are not met – leading to problems with dissatisfied customers/clients.

✓ Junior staff do not have the opportunity to develop new skills – may not be able to deputise if senior staff are unavailable/absent.

7 Describe strategies which could be used to overcome the problem caused by two common time stealers. (4 marks)

> This question is testing your knowledge AND understanding of your study of time and task management.
>
> Your answer should make reference to two of the items below – remember one mark is allocated to each time stealer outlined and one mark for strategies which can be used to avoid them. This is indicated with the use of the dash – separating each statement.

Remember

This question is asking you for suggestions which will help **reduce the effect** of time stealers.

✓ Frequent interruptions whether telephone/visitors – *learn to control time or protect time.*

✓ Unexpected visits by colleagues – *be polite but firm especially if the person is just looking for a chat.*

✓ Meetings that take longer than necessary (face-to-face or on telephone) – *set time limits.*

✓ Taking on too much work – *delegate more tasks, learn to say NO – be assertive.*

✓ Unable to find the information you require – *ensure you have an appropriate filing system.*

✓ Crisis/problematic situations – *have plans in place rather than acting hastily.*

✓ Procrastination – *prioritise your tasks – if tasks prove too difficult, seek help.*

8 An effective leader should have 'good people skills'. Outline four other leadership skills you would expect to see in an effective leader. (4 marks)

> This question is testing your knowledge of your study of team-working. Try not to waste precious time repeating the question four times! For an Outline simply give the examiner a straightforward answer which demonstrates **your** knowledge, for example:
>
> - *An effective leader should have …*
> - *Another skill is the ability to …*
> - *An ability to … would be a very useful skill*
> - *A good leader would be expected to …*

Your answer should include four of the items below:

✓ Good communication skills – written or verbal.

✓ Ability to build trust and relationships within the team.

✓ Ability to listen to ideas so that all the team are included.

✓ Ability to influence others towards the achievement of goals.

✓ Ability to ensure conflict is kept to a minimum.

✓ Ability to deploy team skills effectively.

✓ Have the necessary technical expertise and knowledge required for the job.
✓ Ability to think clearly to anticipate changing priorities.
✓ Ability to analyse problems and results produced.
✓ Ability to delegate tasks to others in the team.
✓ Ability to motivate team members to complete a task effectively.

9 Describe three ways in which a team may be affected by a poor team leader. (6 marks)

This question is testing your understanding of your study of team-working. Therefore, your answer should make reference to three of the items below – remember one mark is allocated to the first part of your answer (outline) and one mark for your second part (*additional point in italics*).

Remember

The question is asking you to describe how a team would be AFFECTED by poor leadership. So your answer should focus on that – take care that you keep referring to the question you are being asked.

✓ The team will be unclear on what they have to do – *as a result resources may be wasted – the job may not be done properly.*
✓ Conflict will exist between team members – *the job may not get done properly.*
✓ The group is unlikely to be motivated – *they will take longer than anticipated to meet their targets.*
✓ Morale will be poor – *there is likely to be a high staff turnover.*
✓ Individuals working separately are less effective than a team – *output will be less.*
✓ A team with poor leadership will not be properly monitored – *likely to do the minimum required/just sufficient to get the job done.*
✓ They are unlikely to be able to work under pressure – *team members will suffer from stress – will be unable to sustain a standard of work for any length of time.*

10 Good teamwork is essential for efficiency and productivity. Discuss reasons why some teams are more effective than others. (6 marks)

This question is also testing your knowledge AND understanding of your study of team-working.

Your answer should cover at least two clearly set out points of information with some exemplification or development.
Make sure there are 'connecting' words which show evidence of discussion: *because, therefore, however, resulting in, on the other hand (good for negatives).* A good idea is to start with a general opening sentence to show you have actually read the question!

✓ Presence of a good leader – helps to promote a positive atmosphere – helps to provide good co-operation between members of the team – skilfully manages conflict.

✓ Team members support one another when working on projects together – leads to better decision making/more risks taken.
✓ Team composition is appropriate to the task – right balance of skills and personalities – appropriate size for the task – too large can cause confusion, but too small could mean a lack of expertise/skill – leads to better productivity/success.
✓ Open and transparent communication between team members – members encouraged to express their opinions/suggest ideas/be prepared to compromise.
✓ All members have a clear idea of what they are there to achieve/ have clear goals/targets.
✓ Teams need to work as a cohesive group/pull together – more targets/deadlines will be met.

11 Outline three strategies an Administrative Assistant could use to comply with the requirements of the Health and Safety Act. (3 marks)

> This question is testing your knowledge of your study of Health and Safety legislation. Your answer should cover three clearly set out points of information.

✓ Ensure that regular breaks are taken.
✓ Change the type of task being done.
✓ Attend Health and Safety training as required.
✓ Comply with Health and Safety guidelines/organisation's policy.
✓ Use safety equipment/clothing provided.
✓ Report faulty equipment.

12 Describe two key responsibilities employers have with regards to Display Screen Equipment regulations. (4 marks)

> This question is also testing your knowledge of your study of Health and Safety legislation. Therefore, your answer should make reference to two of the items below – remember one mark is allocated to the first part of your answer (outline) and one mark for your second part (*additional point in italics*).

Remember

Take care not to repeat a point for an additional mark, for example, prevent injury/RSI.

The question is asking you to describe responsibilities of the employer! Make sure you focus your answer on that.
✓ Ensure that regular screen breaks/ job rotation are taken – *to combat work-related stress.*
✓ Ensure all staff receive the necessary training on how to use the equipment – *to prevent injury such as RSI, back pain, etc.*
✓ Ensure that safety equipment is provided, *for example, wrist rests/ tilting monitors/adjustable chairs.*
✓ To prevent possible injury and, therefore, *no legal action.*
✓ Ensure equipment is maintained *by carrying out regular checks.*

13 Compare the health and safety responsibilities of employers and employees in the workplace. (2 marks)

> This question is testing your knowledge AND understanding of your study of Health and Safety legislation. Therefore, your answer should include two complete statements of comparison or similarity from those listed below.

✓ Employers have a legal responsibility to **provide** a safe working environment and equipment for their employees whereas employees must **use** the equipment provided correctly.

✓ **Employees** have a responsibility to report any hazards they notice to their employer whereas the **employer** has a responsibility to take action (repair) on the hazard as quickly as possible.

✓ Both **employees and employers** have a responsibility to work together to ensure health and safety legislation is complied with.

✓ **Employers** have a responsibility to **risk assess** any dangerous task that employees have to do whereas employees have a responsibility to ensure that they **follow the procedures** that are put in place by employers to reduce risk.

14 Describe the rights of the individual as outlined in the General Data Protection Regulations. (4 marks)

> This question is testing your knowledge and understanding of your study of the General Data Protection Regulations as it applies to the RIGHTS OF THE INDIVIDUAL. Therefore, your answer should make reference to at least two of the items below – remember one mark is allocated to the first part of your answer (outline or statement) and additional marks for your development points (bulleted).

✓ An individual has a right to expect personal details to be used in line with data protection regulations, and that the holder of such details should:
  - get and use the information fairly
  - keep it for only one or more clearly stated and lawful purposes
  - use and make known this information only in ways that are in keeping with these purposes
  - keep the information safe
  - make sure that the information is factually correct, complete and up to date
  - make sure that there is enough information – but not too much – and that it is relevant

- keep the information for no longer than is needed for the reason stated and give an individual a copy of any personal information when asked for it
- disclose the name of the organisation or person collecting the information or for whom they are collecting it
- disclose the reason why they want your details.

15 Outline four methods of good information handling that should be employed by an organisation. (4 marks)

> This question is testing your understanding of the General Data Protection Regulations AND organisational procedures in place to ensure the security of such information. Your answer should make reference to four of the items below.

✓ (An organisation should ensure there are suitable organisational procedures in place):
- Information should be regularly backed up.
- Passwords should be in place to access files.
- A procedure should be in place to ensure passwords are changed regularly.
- An organisation should have appropriate file management systems.
- Information (in hard copy format) should be securely stored or in locked cabinets/rooms.

16 Explain two strategies that could be used to comply with effective data protection handling. (2 marks)

> This type of question, using the command word Explain, is mainly testing your understanding (i.e. the application of your knowledge). In this case, your study of General Data Protection Regulations as it applies to the data users'/handlers' responsibility. Your answer should make reference to two of the items below:

Remember

The command word **Explain** requires you to make connection between cause and effect.

✓ When handling sensitive or confidential data the following strategies could be employed, for example:
- Keep information securely – to reduce the possibility of unauthorised access.
- Confidential/sensitive information must not be passed to a third party without permission – as this could result in legal action.
- Any sensitive/personal information must be kept up to date/accurate – to avoid errors in communication.
- When no longer required, it is important to delete electronic information and shred any hard copy/printed material – to avoid confusion/use of outdated information.

17 Discuss how effective data management can be ensured within an organisation. (6 marks)

> This question is testing your knowledge AND understanding of your study of the impact of IT in the workplace.

✓ It is important that organisations ensure that:
- everyone who needs **access** to data have it but also that people who do not have a right to access, do not
- **log-in procedures** are in force which allow only those authorised to access certain data
- **password protection** is in place – and that staff using passwords are encouraged to change them on a regular basis
- **access rights** are set at different levels including read only, read/write access or no access at all – this could also apply to particular terminals within the workplace
- **data** being sent out are encrypted to prevent them becoming corrupt/hacked, etc.

✓ It is also important that organisations:
- have an **effective backup procedure** in place in case of accidental loss or damage
- **install proper anti-virus software/firewalls** to protect data from being hacked
- **ensure the physical security of hardware** perhaps by having locks on areas where data is managed to discourage theft/ damage, etc.

✓ Organisations should enforce a proper housekeeping policy including:
- providing guidelines/training for staff on file management – having up-to-date user policies in place
- archiving procedures for data no longer required
- putting files in folders with suitable names for easy access on the server
- regular clean-up of individual desk tops i.e. moving them to the server.

Remember

The question is asking you to discuss effective data management – so you need to make reference not only to file management (on the computer) but also physical management – safe storage, etc.

18 Describe the steps that can be taken to make sure that information is managed effectively on a computer network. (3 marks)

> This type of question is testing your knowledge of (electronic) data management skills.
>
> There are three marks available, but the question is asking about steps – plural – so your answer should refer to at least two separate steps. It is a good idea (though not essential) to give a name to the steps you are describing.

Steps (*sometimes referred to as Rules in organisations*) for effective network management can be described as follows:

- ✓ Naming conventions – some organisations will have very strict rules as to the way an electronic file is named – e.g. including the document type (letter/agenda/itinerary), who is the author (managing directors, senior manager), version number if it is a work in progress involving more than one person or department.
- ✓ Create suitable folders – some organisations will have very strict rules as to the way electronic files are grouped together – e.g. by customer or by file type (database or spreadsheet) or by departments.
- ✓ Update regularly – some organisations will have a procedure (weekly/monthly/quarterly/annually) to ensure that data in files is up to date/accurate/deleted/archived if no longer useful or required.

19 Explain the consequences of failing to manage information on a computer network. (4 marks)

> This type of question is testing your understanding of the consequences of poor (electronic) data management skills.
>
> There are four marks available, but the question is asking about consequences – plural – so your answer should refer to at least two separate consequences.

Consequences of failure to manage network data effectively can be explained as follows:

- ✓ If no uniformity or naming conventions are established this could result in information/files being very difficult to find – result in a very stressed/agitated staff – reduce the speed of workflow with resulting loss of output/good customer care, etc.
- ✓ Failure to create suitable folders that follow naming conventions increases the chances of information being lost (breach of General Data Protection Regulations).
- ✓ Updating irregularly – lack of a proper procedure could result in the network becoming overloaded – duplication of information and sometimes meaning staff using the wrong information (not the most up to date).

20 Justify the time taken to manage electronic information. (3 marks)

> This type of question is testing your understanding of the need for good (electronic) data management skills.
>
> There are three marks available and, therefore, three separate justifications (reasons why – use the words because, it means that, it allows, etc.) why organisations should take the time to manage electronic information.

Time should be taken to manage electronic information **because:**

- ✓ it is easier and faster to **find** the information needed, when it is needed
- ✓ it **improves productivity** as staff are not wasting time looking for files
- ✓ it **reduces** the chances of information being lost (breach of GDPR)
- ✓ having a well-organised central system means that all staff are accessing the **most up-to-date** information/files
- ✓ it **saves space** on the network, as duplicate/obsolete files are removed.

21 Describe procedures organisations may put in place to help reduce the risk of information being lost or stolen. (4 marks)

> This type of question is testing your knowledge of (electronic) data protection skills.
>
> There are four marks available, but the question is asking about procedures – plural – so your answer should refer to at least two separate procedures.
>
> It is a good idea (though not essential) to give a name to the procedures you are describing.

- ✓ **Use password protection** – most organisations will have very strict rules regarding username and passwords to allow staff to access electronic data – this allows different levels of access, e.g. assistants may not have access to confidential information that managers may have – strong passwords should have a mixture of letters (upper and lower case), numbers, symbols – passwords need to be updated regularly to reduce the risk of passwords being misused.
- ✓ **Encrypting a device** or file adds another layer of security if files are stolen as a password is required to access any information – it is often company policy that any files being attached to emails or stored on an external device (memory stick) are encrypted.
- ✓ **Installing a firewall** on the computer network – this is a piece of software that reduces the risk of hacking from outside agencies – needs to be kept up to date as hackers are always finding new ways to bypass these security measures.
- ✓ **Installing anti-virus software** – this is a software program which prevents files/systems from being corrupted or destroyed – needs to be kept up to date as hackers are always finding new ways to bypass these security measures.
- ✓ **Organisations** usually have a company policy to help guide staff on how to maintain the security and confidentiality of electronic information – a company may also have a policy on any files being attached to email or stored on an external device (memory stick) – a company may also have a policy on the use of locking screen savers, use of mobile devices, etc. especially if these are being removed from the company premises.

22   Describe the steps that should be taken when taking confidential information out of the office on a portable device. (3 marks)

> This type of question is testing your knowledge of (electronic) data protection skills.
>
> There are three marks available, but the question is asking about steps – plural – so your answer should refer to at least two separate steps – i.e. two steps plus one additional point/example.

- ✓ **Limit the use of external storage devices** – most organisations will have very strict rules regarding the use of memory sticks/pen drives – as information removed from the network can increase the risk of information being lost/corrupted/stolen.
- ✓ **Use password protection** on all mobile devices – most organisations will insist that mobile devices such as tablets or androids have a tracking device installed – to allow them to be located if lost.
- ✓ **Most organisations** will have a policy regarding the procedure to follow – if a mobile device is left unattended/lost while travelling, etc.

23 Explain the consequences of failing to have adequate procedures in place to protect information held on a network. (6 marks)

> This type of question is testing your understanding of the consequences of poor (electronic) data management skills. It is asking for an explanation (a bit more than just describing).
>
> There are six marks available, but the question is asking about consequences – plural – so your answer should refer to at least two separate consequences.

Consequences of failing to have adequate procedures in place to protect network data effectively can be explained as follows:

- ✓ **Data could be accessed by unauthorised persons/personnel** – causing a breaching of the main principles of the General Data Protection Regulations – which could result in a fine – also a loss of faith with the public due to the negative publicity.
- ✓ **Data could be stolen (staff or customer information)** – causing the company to suffer financially, especially if it is sensitive financial data – the company will probably have to pay compensation and take steps to ensure it doesn't happen again.
- ✓ **If no back-ups have been taken** this could result in the information being permanently lost – causing the company to lose custom/sales and ultimately go out of business.

✓ **The company network may have to be completely rebuilt** – the financial cost of which would be very high as a specialist would need to be employed – no business would be able to take place during this period of time.

✓ **The bad publicity the organisation receives may be very difficult to erase** – this can damage the company, particularly their sales as they will lose customers in the short term and may struggle to gain new customers in the longer term.

24 Describe a benefit of flexi-time to (a) the organisation, and (b) the employee. (4 marks)

> This type of question is mainly testing your understanding (i.e. the application of your knowledge). In this case, of your study of working practices as it applies to flexi-time.

(a) The organisation:
- knows that during core-time, the majority of the staff will be there – *allowing meetings and/or training to be organised for this time*
- can allow their staff to start/finish earlier as required – *thus retaining staff who have other responsibilities such as child care*
- benefits from better staff morale – *as staff can choose when to start/finish work.*

(b) The employee:
- can bank extra hours worked – *allowing them to arrange time off if required for personal issues*
- can choose when to start/finish work – *to allow them to deal with responsibilities such as child care*
- benefits from feeling less stressed – *as they can travel outwith rush hour traffic.*

25 Describe the benefits of home-working for an employee. (4 marks)

> This type of question is mainly testing your understanding (i.e. the application of your knowledge). In this case, your understanding of how working practices can be applied to home-working. For four marks your answer should make reference to more than one benefit.

✓ Saves time and expense for the home-worker – *associated with commuting to and from the workplace.*
✓ The home-worker is able to use their own IT equipment – *may be easier to use and less stressful.*
✓ The home-worker can work around other commitments – *by choosing when to start and/or finish work.*
✓ Home-working can lead to increased productivity – *as the home-worker is able to concentrate on the work in hand – fewer distractions/time-stealers/interruptions.*

Remember

To gain full marks you must make reference to both for example:

organisation 3pts, employee 1pt.

26 Discuss the factors regarding IT that need to be considered for employees who want to start working from home. (6 marks)

This question is testing your knowledge AND understanding of your study of the impact of IT on flexible working practices (in this case – home-working). Your answer should cover at least two clearly set out points of information – with words which show evidence of discussion – however, also, it is important that, because, etc.

Take care with this one – don't discuss home-working and the benefits to the employee, for example, 'can enjoy a better work–life balance'. Q25 is the type of question for that. This particular question wants to know the IT factors that the organisation needs to consider to help home-workers perform their work effectively.

Organisation needs to:

✓ ensure that the home-worker has access to the necessary equipment/software – may need to purchase and maintain and/or update equipment/software
✓ consider facilities available in home-worker's area, for example, broadband internet, etc.
✓ provide technical help or support if problems arise
✓ ensure security of equipment in the home
✓ ensure security of information handled by the home-worker
✓ ensure that the home-worker has access to appropriate training
✓ provide access to email to allow communication between the organisation and home-worker – helps to support feeling of isolation relating to working on their own
✓ ensure good health and safety issues by carrying out risk assessment of working in the home.

Remember

Don't be tempted to simply list different hardware/ software – you must exemplify your understanding AND any points made must be related to IT – not family commitments or work–life balance.

Chapter 2 Customer care in administration

1 Describe the benefits of providing good customer service. (3 marks)

This type of question is mainly testing your understanding (i.e. the application of your knowledge). In this case, your understanding of customer service and how it impacts on the organisation.

For three marks your answer should make reference to at least two of the items below. In this type of question – **Describe** command word for three marks – one mark is awarded for each valid description and one mark for each valid development point.

However, **two** marks **maximum** can be awarded for any one **benefit**.

✓ Creates customer loyalty to the organisation – *resulting in increased sales/profit/revenue.*

✓ Customers will tell others about the good customer service which will improve the reputation of the organisation – *give the organisation a competitive edge/increase market share.*

✓ A good reputation for the organisation can increase staff morale which could have a positive effect on recruitment/result in increased sales, etc.

✓ Increased staff morale may result in lower staff turnover – *reducing recruitment costs of the organisation.*

✓ Good customer service will result in fewer complaints to employees from customers – *resulting in a happier workforce.*

Remember

Take care not to continue to use increase in profit/sales/revenue as this will only be given one mark for the first time you use it.

2 Explain the consequences of poor customer service. (5 marks)

> This type of question is also testing your understanding (i.e. the application of your knowledge) of customer care. However, in this instance the consequences of not providing good customer care and the impact on the organisation.
>
> It is important that you show understanding of cause and effect by providing a number of straightforward points of explanation or a smaller number of developed points or a combination of both – depending on the marks available.
>
> One mark will be awarded for each relevant point of explanation and another mark for a further development point – which could be an example of the effect.

✓ Customers **will tell others** about the bad customer service which could:
- destroy the reputation of the organisation
- decrease sales/revenue/profit
- decrease market share.

✓ A bad reputation for the organisation can **decrease staff morale** which could:
- have a negative effect on recruitment
- result in decreased sales, etc.

✓ Decreased staff morale may result in **higher staff turnover**:
- increasing stress levels for remaining staff
- increasing recruitment costs of the organisation
- making it difficult to attract quality staff.

✓ Bad customer service will result **in more complaints** to employees from customers:
- resulting in an unhappy workforce
- demotivating the workforce.

✓ Decreases or **destroys customer loyalty** to the organisation resulting in:
- customers taking their business elsewhere
- decreased sales/profit/revenue.

3 Outline the features of an effective complaints procedure.
(4 marks)

> This type of question is testing your knowledge of the contents of an effective complaints procedure within an organisation.
>
> Try not to waste time repeating the question four times. For an outline, simply give the examiner a straightforward list which demonstrates your knowledge.
>
> Your answer should include any four of the following items.

The features of an effective complaints procedure:

- ✓ The details of the person or department in charge of complaints should be provided.
- ✓ The most effective timescale for dealing with complaints should be outlined.
- ✓ The same person should handle the complaint from start to finish.
- ✓ Formal written complaints should be acknowledged in writing immediately/by return.
- ✓ Verbal complaints should be logged when received – either face to face or by telephone.
- ✓ Complaints by social media should be acknowledged.
- ✓ Customer should be given details of how the complaint can be dealt with or how the problem can be resolved.
- ✓ The process should be monitored by senior staff member.
- ✓ Each complaint should be treated on its own merit.
- ✓ Each complaint should be treated as high priority.

4 Describe two methods of gathering customer feedback.
(4 marks)

> This type of question is testing your knowledge of customer care and of the procedures that need to be in place within an organisation to gather customer feedback.
>
> The question is very specific and requires your answer to make reference to two of the items below. One mark is awarded for each valid method described and one mark for any additional comment, illustration or example.

- ✓ **Written survey:** for example, a pre-printed form or questionnaire posted out to customers to enable them to reply (with pre-paid envelope – FREEPOST address) with their thoughts on the service received.

✓ **Telephone survey:** for example, contacting customers and asking a series of pre-set questions to enable them to reply on a one-to-one basis on the service received (sometimes outsourced to call centres).

✓ **Comment cards:** containing pre-set short questions with tick boxes (rating 1–5) – easy to complete by customers (but have to be stored/collated by administrative staff).

✓ **Online survey:** a questionnaire containing a series of questions which is completed online – simple and easy for customers to use and data collected can be stored and collated easily.

✓ **Customer focus group:** a meeting of a representative sample of customers to discuss the service received/provided – feedback is immediate and can provide a platform for more in-depth discussion.

✓ **Mystery shopper:** employees who act as a normal customer who then report back on the service they have received – either good or bad – and praise given if good and action (training, etc.) taken if bad.

5 Compare electronic methods of gathering customer feedback to more traditional face-to-face or paper-based systems.
(2 marks)

This question is testing your knowledge AND understanding of your study of evaluating customer service standards.

Your answer should include two complete statements of comparison or similarities from those listed below.

✓ Written survey requires customers to fill in a paper questionnaire and return it using an envelope **whereas** an online survey only requires the customer to use the mouse to complete the survey and it is automatically saved to the company website.

✓ Telephone/one-to-one survey allows customers to ask questions before responding **whereas** an online survey only provides set answers for customers from which to select responses.

✓ Written survey requires the organisation to manually record (key-in), save and analyse the data from the questionnaire **whereas** an online survey automatically records, saves and analyses data.

✓ **Both methods** allow the findings to be saved for future reference.

✓ Review sites allow customers to give their ratings for a product/service immediately **whereas** a written survey takes more time to process to become effective information.

✓ **Both methods** can be outsourced to specialist marketing organisations.

Remember

The question is asking you to compare electronic and traditional methods of gathering customer feedback including similarities – i.e. features which apply to BOTH!

Chapter 3 Effectively manage information

1 Describe methods of communication that could be used during induction training. (3 marks)

> This type of question is testing your knowledge of the types of communication used within the administrative function.
>
> The question is very specific and requires your answer to make reference to induction training – and you should make reference to more than one as the question specifies 'methods' (plural).
>
> One mark is awarded for each valid method described – plus one mark for any additional comment, illustration or example. In other words, three separate points or two points, one of which needs an additional point.

✓ **Written** communication in the form of a **leaflet** summarising the information being communicated – it is a fairly cheap method to produce – it can be printed or uploaded to the network – as it is a written document it can be saved and referred to as required.

✓ **Written** communication in the form of a **poster** displaying the information being communicated – it needs to use a mixture of graphics and text to grab the reader's attention – it can be printed and displayed on a notice board for easy referral as required.

✓ **Face-to-face** communication in the form of a **PowerPoint presentation** where the presenter communicates information to more than one person at a time using slides projected on a screen – graphics and audio files can be attached to grab the audience and make the information more memorable – notes can be produced for the audience to keep for future reference.

✓ **Face-to-face** communication in the form of a **meeting** where smaller groups can be brought together to share and discuss information – allows for easier question and answer sessions to be done more efficiently.

✓ **Face-to-face** communication in the form of a **video conference/ meeting** where groups can be brought together from different geographical areas (e.g. head office and various branch offices) to share and discuss information – saves expense of travel and accommodation which would be required otherwise.

2 Compare written methods with face-to-face methods of communication. (3 marks)

> This question is testing your knowledge AND understanding of your study of communication within the administrative function.
>
> Your answer should include three complete statements of comparison from those listed below.

Remember

The question is asking you to compare written and face-to-face methods of communication including similarities, that is, features which apply to BOTH!

✓ Written communication in the form of an information leaflet needs to be printed and may become out of date whereas a face-to-face meeting can be informal, requiring no printed material, allowing the most up-to-date information to be passed on.

✓ Written communication in the form of an information poster can be ignored after being displayed for some time whereas a face-to-face meeting ensures that the audience is engaged in the information/discussion process at the time.

✓ Written methods of communication can be ignored (e.g. email) whereas a face-to-face method (e.g. a meeting) ensures participation in the process.

✓ Both written and face-to-face methods allow information being communicated to be saved for future reference (emails/posters/leaflets and PowerPoint presentation notes printed or electronically saved).

3 Discuss the advantages and disadvantages of using electronic methods of communication. (6 marks)

> This type of question is testing your knowledge and understanding of electronic communication.
>
> Although not essential it is better to name the type of electronic communication being discussed, for example: email, text message, etc.
>
> One mark is awarded for each valid discussion point.
>
> Your answer should cover at least six clearly set out points of information – with words which show evidence of discussion – **however, also, it is important that, because**, etc.

Remember

The question uses the Discuss command word and requires relevant and accurate points but with an element of discussion within each point. This is made easier because the question is looking for advantages and disadvantages specifically.

✓ Email can be sent to multiple users at the one time which saves time (Adv). However, because the emails are being sent to more than one person, they are sometimes ignored because they are not perceived as important and/or require a reply (Disadv). (2 marks)

✓ Email can have attachments added such as documents, spreadsheets, presentations or pictures which allows very specific information to be communicated (Adv); however, this can result in sensitive information being seen by unauthorised users/being hacked (Disadv). (2 marks)

✓ Email can be accessed on mobile devices (Adv) – so even if people are out and about they can receive, read and respond to email messages (Adv). (2 marks)

✓ Emails are an ideal form of communicating simple messages (Adv); however, if the contents become complex and need further explanation/discussion email is possibly not the best choice and a face-to-face meeting may be required (Disadv). (2 marks)

✓ Instant messaging allows staff to get in touch quickly where a meeting or phone call is not necessary/would interrupt workflow (Adv).

✓ Instant messaging allows one-to-one discussions or group chats (Adv).

✓ Social media platforms (Twitter, Facebook, etc) allow a more informal method of communication as messages tend to be short and/or limited in size (Adv). However, there is no guarantee that everyone will see the message if they do not check their accounts regularly (Disadv). Also if there are too many posts on a particular subject, the message can easily get lost (Disadv). (3 marks) Because the information posted on **social media sites** is open to the public, staff, etc. need to be very careful about what information is posted (Disadv).

✓ **Video-conferencing** allows people from all over the world to meet without the need to travel (Adv). However, technical difficulties can arise, for example, connectivity issues can cause many problems for the users (Disadv). (2 marks)

✓ **Mobile devices like laptops, tablets and mobile phones** are increasingly used, but running out of battery power can result in loss of communication (Disadv).

4 Justify the use of an e-diary when an Administrative Assistant is arranging a formal meeting. (2 marks)

> This type of question is testing your understanding of the need for good electronic methods of arranging a meeting.
>
> There are two marks available, and you should therefore give two separate justifications, i.e. reasons why an Administrative Assistant would use an e-diary when arranging a meeting. Try to use the words **because**, **it means that**, **it allows**, etc.

An Administrative Assistant would use an e-diary to arrange a meeting because:

✓ It is easy and quick to invite delegates/attendees as other e-diaries can be checked to find a suitable date when all or most are available.

✓ It allows invited attendees to reply immediately whether they can attend or send their apologies for absence.

✓ It allows the Administrative Assistant to set up automatic alerts to remind attendees of the date and time of the meeting.

✓ It allows the Administrative Assistant to enter recurring (e.g. monthly) meetings automatically – including automatic reminders of the date and time of the meeting.

5 Compare the use of audio-conferencing with web-conferencing. (2 marks)

> This question is testing your knowledge AND understanding of your study of the impact of IT in the workplace. Therefore, your answer should include two complete statements of comparison or similarities from the following.

✓ Audio-conferencing uses verbal communication only **whereas** web-conferencing (video-conferencing) allows for both audio and visual communication.

✓ Web-conferencing can show facial expressions/body language which is useful for interviews **whereas** audio-conferencing is limited to the spoken word only.

✓ Audio-conferencing uses only a microphone and loudspeaker **whereas** web-conferencing will use a webcam/digital camera in addition.

✓ **Both** can save travel and accommodation costs – including time spent travelling and being away from the workplace.

✓ **Both** can allow group discussions and meetings to take place from different locations, for example, between branches like Glasgow and Edinburgh.

✓ **Both** may be recorded for future reference.

Remember

The question is asking you to compare responsibilities of employers AND employees including similarities – i.e. features which apply to BOTH!

6 Describe the barriers that may exist when communicating information to others. (3 marks)

> This type of question is testing your knowledge of the barrier to effective communication within the administrative function.
>
> There are three marks, but the question is asking about barriers – plural – so your answer should refer to at least two separate barriers – i.e. one point plus an additional point and a separate point.

Barriers to communication can be described as follows:

✓ **Cultural** or **language** barriers as business is increasingly international can cause information to be misunderstood – especially if the language being used is not the presenter's or the delegate's first language.

✓ The **accent** of the presenter may make the information being delivered difficult to understand.

✓ **Lack of interest** due to:
  ● presentations and/or meetings being too long
  ● written information being too long or detailed.

✓ **Noise** can be a real distraction to hearing what is being communicated.

✓ **Jargon** can be a real problem making what is being communicated difficult to understand.

✓ **Information overload** can be a real barrier to hearing what is being communicated as delegates/staff can become overwhelmed by the amount of information – leading to stress and demotivation.

✓ **Technical difficulties** can be a physical barrier preventing information being communicated at all – sound equipment failing – projector not working – links in presentations not working (network failure), battery power failing, etc.

7 Describe strategies that can be used to avoid the barriers that you provided in Question 6. (3 marks)

> This type of question is testing your understanding of the importance of poor communication skills.
>
> There are three marks, but the question is asking about barriers – plural – so your answer should refer to at least two separate barriers – i.e. one point plus an additional point and a separate point.

Strategies to avoid the barriers to communication can be described as follows:

✓ **Cultural/language (accent)** barriers – provide support (from a language specialist) who can gauge when understanding is being lost – who can stop a presentation to ask relevant questions or clarify points.

✓ **Lack of interest** due to presentations and/or meetings being too long can be avoided by – ensuring meetings are well-structured and organised – giving a short (comfort) break to allow the audience to move – build in discussion groups to limit the amount of time the audience have to be quiet and listen.

✓ **Lack of interest** due to written information being too long or detailed – can be avoided by reducing the amount of continuous text within a document – make use of diagrams and graphics to convey information more easily – avoid very long web pages by the use of hyperlinks rather than scrolling down to read information.

✓ **Noise** can be avoided by ensuring if the room is large that the presenter has a microphone – asking the audience for quiet – using air-conditioning rather than opening windows (especially in a city location) – placing notices requesting quiet outside the meeting room – relocating the venue if there is going to be noisy work being done outside of the building or within the building itself.

✓ **Jargon** – can be avoided by issuing a glossary of difficult or specialised words or phrases beforehand for reference – simply avoiding the use of mnemonics and/or technical words that only specialists understand.

✓ **Information overload** can be avoided by simply limiting the amount of information being communicated at any one time – have several shorter meetings rather than one really long meeting – distribute leaflets outlining the main points (summarising) the information being communicated.

✓ **Technical difficulties** can be overcome by always having a back-up plan in place (needs organisation) – ensure paper copies of the electronic information are available should there be a loss of power – check all hyperlinks etc. are working before the meeting takes place.

8 Describe the consequences of possible communication barriers during a presentation with a large number of people in the audience. (4 marks)

> This type of question is testing your understanding of the consequences of poor communication skills.
>
> There are four marks available, but the question is asking about consequences – plural – so your answer should refer to at least two separate consequences.

Consequences of possible communication barriers can be described as follows:

✓ **The session may need to be stopped/adjourned** – resulting in wasted time for the organisation as another date will need to be set – this will inconvenience the employees who may have to travel and are not able to return – can result in additional travel and accommodation costs/arrangements.

✓ **Cultural/language barriers could result in the attendees not fully understanding what is being said** – could result in legal action being taken (e.g. if something is taken out of context) – could damage the reputation of the organisation (for the same reason) – could have a negative effect on people's ability to do their job.

✓ **Interruptions/distractions/noise, etc.** – could result in a very agitated audience, causing stress or lack of interest – resulting in bad decisions being made/wrong or misunderstood information taken away.

✓ **If the presentation is because of a legal requirement of the job** – could result in fines and legal action being taken against the organisation – e.g. people working with children (child protection training) or people dealing with sensitive information (data protection training).

Final IT assignment – a worked example

The following assignment is based on the standards outlined in the Course Assessment Specification produced by SQA for CfE Higher Administration and IT. Each task includes a 'How to!' section to help you tackle future assignments.

Remember, the final assignment is done under examination conditions and is also timed – so you need to make sure that you can easily perform the functions you have learned during your classwork and revision. If you become expert at these (that means do them without having to stop and wonder what you did last October!) it should mean that you can tackle the 'problem-solving' aspect of the Assignment with much more confidence – leading to achieving the maximum marks available.

Do each part of this assignment (especially the parts you find more difficult) as many times as possible – this will build up brain muscle memory!

Seaview Academy

You work as an Administrative Assistant in the school office of Seaview Academy in Portpatrick.

One of your main duties is to help staff plan and organise trips for pupils. The Humanities Faculty runs various trips every year and at the moment you are helping Gavin Fallow, History Teacher in the Humanities Faculty, organise a three-day trip to Newcastle at end of the last term. Ana Geissman, Business Education, is helping Gavin with the preparations.

The main focus of the trip is to visit Beamish, the North of England Open Air Museum in County Durham, England. Pupils will also have the opportunity to visit the Namco Funscape in Newcastle.

Remember

This section sets the scene and gives information you will need to complete all of the tasks to the highest level, for example, who you are doing the tasks for — for a reference in a letter perhaps. Make sure you read it and highlight any information you may think is important.

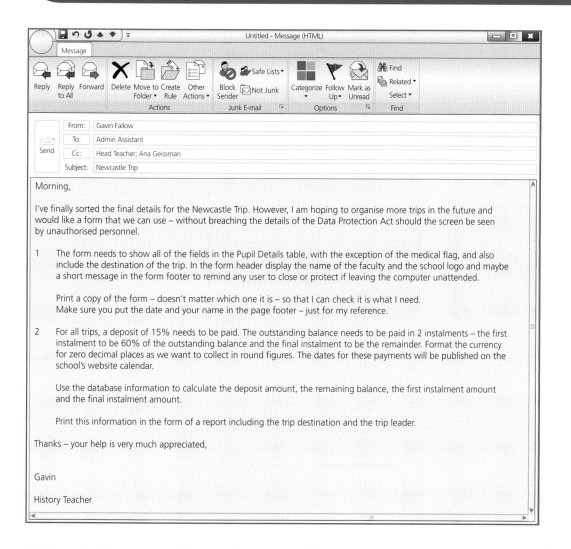

Morning,

I've finally sorted the final details for the Newcastle Trip. However, I am hoping to organise more trips in the future and would like a form that we can use – without breaching the details of the Data Protection Act should the screen be seen by unauthorised personnel.

1   The form needs to show all of the fields in the Pupil Details table, with the exception of the medical flag, and also include the destination of the trip. In the form header display the name of the faculty and the school logo and maybe a short message in the form footer to remind any user to close or protect if leaving the computer unattended.

Print a copy of the form – doesn't matter which one it is – so that I can check it is what I need. Make sure you put the date and your name in the page footer – just for my reference.

2   For all trips, a deposit of 15% needs to be paid. The outstanding balance needs to be paid in 2 instalments – the first instalment to be 60% of the outstanding balance and the final instalment to be the remainder. Format the currency for zero decimal places as we want to collect in round figures. The dates for these payments will be published on the school's website calendar.

Use the database information to calculate the deposit amount, the remaining balance, the first instalment amount and the final instalment amount.

Print this information in the form of a report including the trip destination and the trip leader.

Thanks – your help is very much appreciated,

Gavin

History Teacher

This is a database task. Before you begin to tackle any database task it is a good idea to either print out the Relationship Report or simply just open it from the Database Tools Ribbon. This will help when looking for the table which stores the information you need.

- The first part of this task is testing your ability to create a **form** – enhancing it with graphics and/or text. You also need to print one record (to prove you can do it – I know it sounds silly but that is the only reason to print a form) and it needs to have your name in the page footer (**NOT** the form footer).
- The second part of the task is testing your ability to create new fields within a query – an Expression – so that calculations can be made to insert into a report. Make sure you have practised as many different types of calculations as possible.

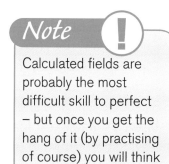

Note

Calculated fields are probably the most difficult skill to perfect – but once you get the hang of it (by practising of course) you will think it is easy!

How to!

The first part of this task requires you to create a form from more than one table to be used to insert data into a database – the **Pupil Details** and the **Trip Details**. The order you choose has an impact on the final form – however, the more you practise the better you will be able to either make the correct choice right away or edit it in Design view. Remember it is a wizard and if you get into a huge mess just get rid of it and start again (much quicker, honestly).

- From the Create Ribbon, select Form Wizard and select either the Pupils or the Trip details table from the drop-down ▼ menu in the first dialogue box.
- Select Trip from the Trip Details Table using the > symbol.
- Select the Pupil Details Table as before, and select all items EXCEPT Medical Flag – the task specifically asked that – **Hint** select all using the **>>** symbol and then de-select Medical Flag using the **<** symbol – it's a bit quicker.

- The next dialogue box may display the form viewed from the Trip Details table, i.e. showing that there would be a sub-form included. For the purposes of this task, it would not be suitable as it would display more than one record at a time.

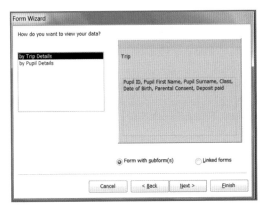 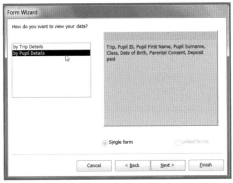

- Select the option to view by Pupil Details – and the box will show a Single form view.
- Click Next **>**, then Columnar Form
- Click Next **>** and key-in 'Humanities Faculty' in the Title Box – remember you were told to include that as a form header.
- Select Design View and Insert the logo in the form header as requested.

- Insert a suitable text form footer to display a warning notice about leaving the computer unattended, using **Aa** label from the Form Design Tools Ribbon.
- Insert today's date in the page footer (remember, right-click and select Page Header/Footer from the pop-up menu) using the **ab|** text box and keying-in the formula =Now() in the Unbound Box – increase the size of the box so that there is enough space to display the date – if there is not enough space ##### will be displayed instead of the date. Change the Properties of this box to Short date. (Right-click on the box and select the Properties option at the very bottom of the pop-up menu.)

- Delete the Text box as it isn't needed in this case.
- Insert your name and centre using **Aa** label.

- IF there is time, enhance the form, for example:
  - Change the background of the header and footer to white.
  - Enhance the entry boxes using colour and special effects.

The final form should look something like this →

Remember, when printing use the mouse to activate selected records in the Print dialogue box you only want to print one – not 75!

The next part of this task requires you to **Create** a Query to be used to insert some new fields – Expressions – so that calculations can be done for a report. Creating the query first means all of the hard work is done and the report can be done using the wizard.

- From the Create Ribbon, select Query Design and select the Teacher Details and Trip Details tables only (the information you need is stored in these two tables).
- Select the following fields – Trip, First Name, Surname, Trip Leader (key-in Yes and de-select the 'Show' option), Cost per Pupil.
- Select the ∑ Totals option from the Design Tools – Total: Group By will appear.
- In the next blank field key-in the label you want (Deposit followed by a colon) and the calculation, i.e. 15% of the Cost. Remember to use square brackets [] around the **Field Name** (syntax).

```
Deposit:[Cost per Pupil]*.15
```

- Select **Expression** from the pop-up menu ▾. You need to do this if you want to use this new field in another calculation.

The task requires you to format the field for currency and 0 decimal places.
- Select Property Sheet from the Query Design Tools Ribbon (OR right-click on the field and at the bottom of the pop-up menu, select Properties), Format > Currency, Decimal places > 0.
- In the next blank field key-in the label Outstanding Balance: and the calculation you need to perform, i.e. Cost less Deposit.

```
Outstanding Balance:[Cost per Pupil]-[Deposit]
```

- In the next blank field key-in the label **First Instalment:** and the calculation you need to perform, i.e. 60% of the Outstanding Balance.

```
First Instalment:[Outstanding Balance]*.6
```

- In the next blank field key-in the label **Final Instalment:** and the calculation you need to perform, i.e. Outstanding Balance less First Instalment.

```
Final Instalment:[Outstanding Balance]-[First
Instalment]
```

The final Design View for this Query is shown below.

- Close and Save this query with a sensible name – Calculation data for Report.
- Select Report Wizard from the Create Ribbon.
- Follow the steps as you would normally (all fields are needed from the Query EXCEPT Trip Leader – as this was necessary only for the search).
- As there are only four trips choose landscape. Also you need a suitable heading – just say what you see! – Financial Details for School Trips.
- Delete the Label for Surname (in the page header – not the Detail!) and Rename the First Name label to Trip Leader.
- IF there is time – revisit the report and enhance it with colour (if you have a colour printer), font types, styles, size, etc. – see Design View.

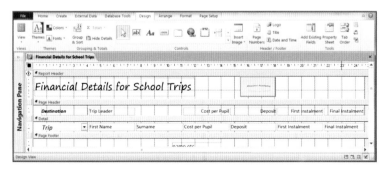

Hi, I've started a letter for the parents about the arrangements for the Newcastle trip – can you finish it and print out one copy of the completed letter for me to check. Firstly, change History Department to Humanities Faculty wherever it appears.

Can you insert a subject heading – including the name of the trip. Before the paragraph outlining the payments schedule, can you add the following (in bulleted list form):

This trip is inclusive of – coach travel, two nights' bed and breakfast, dinner on each evening, entry into Beamish Museum, lunch at both Beamish and Funscape.

The letter should have a Consent Form as a final page – landscape format – and should include – name of trip, space for name and class of pupil, parent/guardian signature and date, a tick box to indicate that parents give their consent that this extra trip is OK with them, and finally a space where pupils can indicate their first and second choice of extra activities available in the evenings. Finally, insert the school logo in the right-hand side of the footer of any pages that don't have it elsewhere.

This is a word processor task. Remember your name should appear on all pages. This task is:

- Testing your ability to (quickly) edit a WP document to enhance it making sure that you use a consistent layout and presentation.
- Testing your ability to use different types of page breaks, and Headers and Footers.
- Testing your ability to insert graphics and/or watermarks.
- It is also testing your skills in using comments in electronic files.

How to!

- Open the Document and Remove Watermark.
- Insert suitable reference – GF/your own initials.
- Insert today's date – both of these before the Salutation and watch your spacing is consistent.
- Work through the Comments – Use the Review Ribbon, Comments section – Delete Comment, Next. If you use this system you won't miss any comments.

Now work through the task as specified.

- Use Replace Option on the Editing section of the Home Ribbon – i.e. replace History Department with Humanities Faculty.
- Insert Subject Heading below Salutation – use bold or ALL CAPITALS.

Hints & tips

Make sure you use the ¶ Show/Hide so that you know where your breaks, etc. are placed on the document.

- Insert the information from the Spreadsheet Summary sheet as requested. Sort into alphabetical order FIRST then Convert Table to Text. These functions are all in the Data Section of the Table Tools Layout Tab.
- You should probably insert a Break > Section Break > Next Page before this section rather than having a break in the middle of the list.
- After the Department at the bottom of the letter, press return twice and key-in – Enc – to signify that there is an enclosure (the consent form).
- You must insert a Break > Section Break > Next Page before this section – as you want the extra page to be landscape.

This part of the task should make full use of the page – you will lose the presentation mark if it doesn't.

It should include:

- The name and address of the school and school logo.
- The name of the trip (larger font to make it stand out).
- Insert a table (for example, 4 columns x 2 rows) and resize each cell to fit the information.
- Format headers and footers as requested.

The finished document should look something like this. Note page 1 is not numbered and page 2 has school logo in the footer. Also name, etc. is in the header – it is simply there to prove to the examiner that it is your own work.

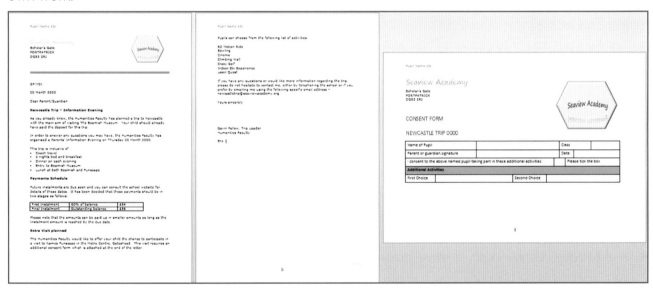

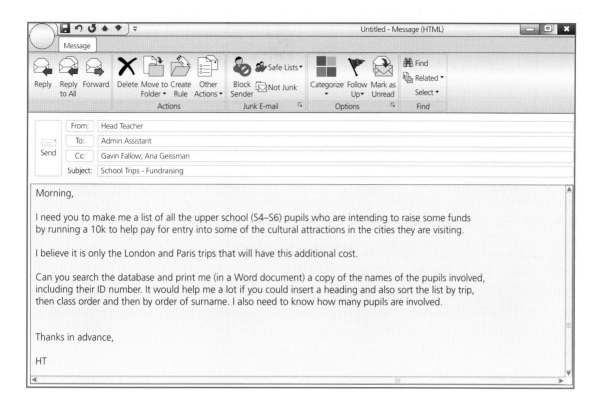

This is a database task. This task is testing your ability to search a database by creating a Query using different criteria. It is also testing your ability to export to a Word document and your knowledge of tables in word processing.

How to!

The first part of this task requires you to Create a Query – from more than one table.

- From the Create Ribbon, select Create Query and select the Pupils Details and the Trip Details table.
- Select Pupil ID, Pupil First Name and Pupil Surname, then Class and Trip.
- In the 'Class' field criteria, key-in:

`4* or 5* or 6* and press the Tab or Return key`	No need to key in anything else

- In the 'Trip' field, criteria, key-in:

`London or Paris and press the Tab or Return key`	No need to key in anything else

- Save using a sensible filename, for example, Fundraising upper school only.

The design view of the query is shown with the syntax in place on page 140 – the program automatically changes what you have keyed-in – so no worries there.

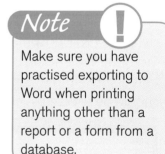

Note

Make sure you have practised exporting to Word when printing anything other than a report or a form from a database.

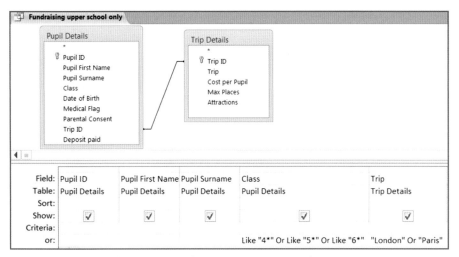

Field: Pupil ID, Pupil First Name, Pupil Surname, Class, Trip

Field:	Pupil ID	Pupil First Name	Pupil Surname	Class	Trip
Table:	Pupil Details	Pupil Details	Pupil Details	Pupil Details	Trip Details
Sort:					
Show:	✓	✓	✓	✓	✓
Criteria:					
or:				Like "4*" Or Like "5*" Or Like "6*"	"London" Or "Paris"

- You now need to Export this query to a Word Document.
- From the External Data Ribbon, Export section select Word from the More ▼ option.
- Select where you want the document to be automatically saved – click on the Browse option to do this. Make sure you save to the folder you are working from – or you will not be able to find it later! Select

☑ **Open the destination file after the export operation is complete.**
Select this option to view the results of the export operation. This option is available only when you export formatted data.

Word will automatically open a word processing document in Rich Text Format (Compatibility Mode). This is a document with the extension .rtf.

- From the Page Layout Ribbon, Page Setup, Size ▼ select A4 – (the default for RTF documents is Letter size).
- From the Table Tools, Layout Ribbon select Sort and the three options as requested in the task – note that the 'Header row' radio button should be selected.

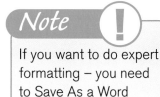

Note
If you want to do expert formatting – you need to Save As a Word document – .docx

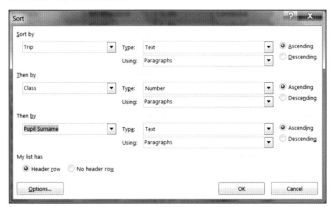

- From the Table Tools Layout Ribbon, select Autofit ▼ Contents.
- Insert a row above the top of the table, merge the cells and key-in a suitable heading.
- Merge the two cells containing Pupil First Name and Pupil Surname – Replace headings with Name (left align).
- Insert a row below the last row (press Tab in the final cell) and merge the first three cells then key-in – 'Total Number of Pupils' (right align this cell).
- In the second last cell (Class column) select *fx* Formula option from the Layout Ribbon and the dialogue box will appear.

- Overwrite SUM and key-in COUNT and the formula should read =COUNT(ABOVE).
- Click OK and the number of entries (i.e. number of pupils) in the column above will be displayed.
- Shade the last cell (as it is blank) and shade any others you think will look good.

The final table should look like this:

Names of Pupils Fundraising for London and Paris Trips				
Pupil ID	Name		Class	Trip
3	Phoebe	Cairns	4.1	London
4	Morgan	Corrigan	4.1	London
7	Robert	Hannah	5.2	London
9	Peter	King	5.4	London
10	Shannon	Malcolm	5.2	London
13	Kimberley	McIntyre	4.2	London
17	Robyn	Russell	5.2	London
18	Matthew	Stevenson	6.1	London
19	Kay	Wild	6.1	London
22	Steven	Campbell	6.1	London
24	Matthew	Drysdale	6.1	London
31	John	McDowell	6.1	London
32	Julie	McKie	6.1	London
43	Shannon	Ferguson	5.2	London
45	Michaela	Hendry	5.1	London
47	Jon	Leslie	5.3	London
50	Kieran	Costley	5.3	London
51	Sophie	McMaster	5.3	London
53	Vicky	Packer	5.2	London
57	Jordan	Wright	5.1	London
62	Natasha	Rennie	6.1	London
65	Shona	Johnstone	4.3	London
68	Rory	McCulloch	5.1	London
70	Cameron	Garrity	5.3	London
16	Fergus	Phillips	5.2	Paris
27	Eric	Hutton	6.1	Paris
29	Fraser	Mann	5.3	Paris
38	James	Wilson	6.1	Paris
44	James	Greenhill	4.2	Paris
46	George	Jackson	5.1	Paris
49	Bobby	McCready	5.3	Paris
58	Joanne	Barker	4.2	Paris
Total Number of Pupils			32	

Hi

I have started to plan for pupils while they are on the Newcastle Trip in the SS File named – Costings.

Could you help me work out the figures? I only need them for the Newcastle Trip at the moment.

Pupils have made their choices, but I need to work out how much they need to pay in the Newcastle Worksheet.

Print a value view on one page and a formulae view on one page.

I also need to send a copy of the total costs so that the office can get the money ready to go with each group leader to pay on the day. Can you complete and print the summary worksheet so I can pass it to the office? We will also qualify for some discounts – depending on the number going – so I have included this information in the worksheet to help with the calculations.

Print formulae view on one page – don't print the discount information.

Thanks, Gavin

Hints & tips ⭐

See Chapter 4 on spreadsheets – before starting Page Setup.

This is a spreadsheet task. Remember to use the Page Layout dialogue box to put your name, etc. on the sheets you are going to print.

- This task is testing your ability to select the correct function and then apply it quickly – using the Function Palette.
- It is also testing your skills in using 3D formulae to complete a Summary Sheet.

Hints & tips ⭐

Make sure you know the different functions – when looking for Price it is usually a V or H Lookup.

How to!

To put the correct price in each cell, check the data first – in this case the PRICES sheet in the SS workbook – it is a vertical list so it will need a VLOOKUP function.

Using the mouse, select the data as shown – remember to press F4 when selecting the Table_Array (PRICES sheet).

- To find the exact match (*i.e. the correct price*) make sure you key-in false in the Range_lookup section.

For the second part of this task, select the SUMMARY sheet. To count how many of each activity and to add up how much it will cost use the COUNTIF and SUMIF functions from the *fx* palette.

- Select cell B4 and the COUNTIF Function Arguments.
- Using the mouse, select the data Range from the NEWCASTLE sheet as shown – remember to press F4 to 'lock' the data selected.

- Use the tab key to select the **Criteria Argument**, and select cell A4 in the SUMMARY sheet.
- Using the mouse, select the data **Sum_ range** from the NEWCASTLE sheet as shown – remember to press F4 to 'lock' the data selected.
- Fill both down – format currency where required.

For the third part of this task, stay in the SUMMARY sheet. To calculate the Price less any discount which may apply, IF Function Arguments from the *fx* palette.

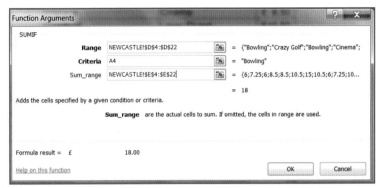

The criteria for applying a discount is:

- In Cell D4 select IF Function.
- Use the mouse to Select B4 and the keyboard to key-in >10 (always start at highest).
- Use the Tab key and **Value_if_True** and using the mouse select/key-in:

```
C4-(C4*$G$6)       i.e. Total less (10% of the Total)
```

- Use the Tab key and in the **Value_if_False** section, select IF from the Formula bar.
- Repeat the previous step – except key-in >3 and select cell **G5**.

```
C4-(C4*$G$5)       i.e. Total less (5% of the Total)
```

- Use the Tab key and in the **Value_if_false** section use the mouse to select C4 – i.e. no discount just the Total.

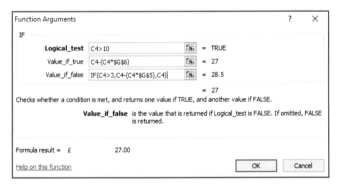

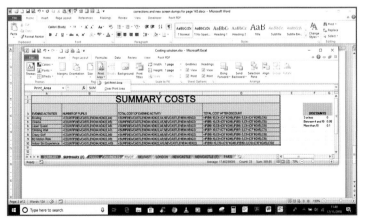

Hints & tips

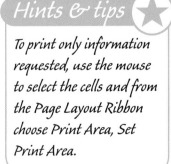

To print only information requested, use the mouse to select the cells and from the Page Layout Ribbon choose Print Area, Set Print Area.

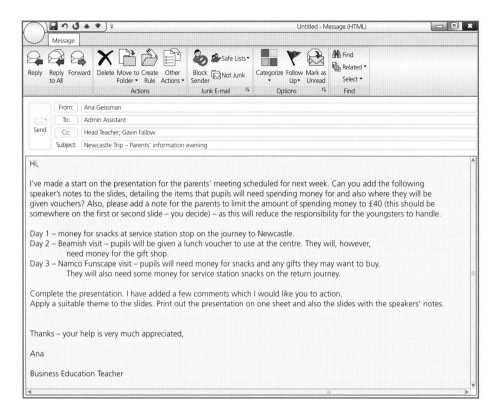

This is a presentation task (using PowerPoint or similar). Remember to use the Insert Ribbon to put your name, etc. on all printouts. You can also put your name on each slide – or the name of the presenter.

- This task is testing your ability to (quickly) edit a presentation to enhance it – using Master slide View.
- AND, testing your ability to print in different formats – slides/ speaker notes, etc.
- It is also testing your skills in using comments in electronic files.

Hints & tips

Make sure you know how to use the View > Master Slides options when putting graphics, etc. ON ALL SLIDES.

How to!

- To add your name to all slides and handouts, simply select Insert Ribbon> Header and Footer and complete as requested.

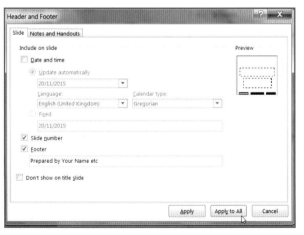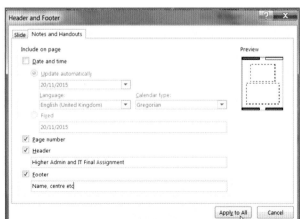

- Remember to use BOTH tabs and Apply to all.
- To Add a Theme – i.e. a background – do this FIRST – using View Ribbon > Slide Master > Themes. (You should have done this many times in class at N4/5 level as well as Higher.)

- To put a graphic quickly on all slides also use the View Ribbon > Slide Master. Select the slides you want (Title, Title and content and Blank slide master) and copy and paste the logo in a suitable place.
- To add speaker's notes – simply go to 'Click to add notes' at the bottom of the window and key-in detail as instructed – it is also a good idea to increase the size of the font to at least 14 so it's easier for the speaker to read.
- The space below can be adjusted to suit by dragging the line between the slide and the notes section up or down.
- Printing as requested – do this in the Print Dialogue box, for example, six slides to a page, OR Notes Pages, for example, 2–5 (the only slides with speaker's notes).

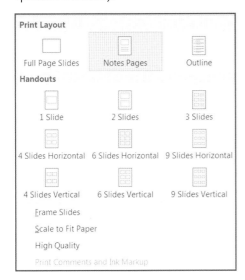

Print Slides 6 per page

header and footer as specified

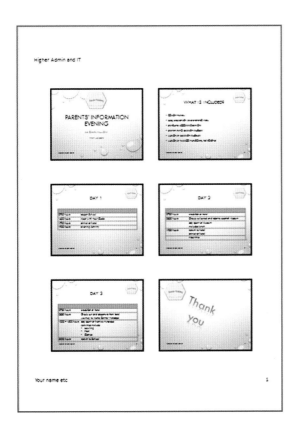

Print Notes page (2–5)

header and footer as specified

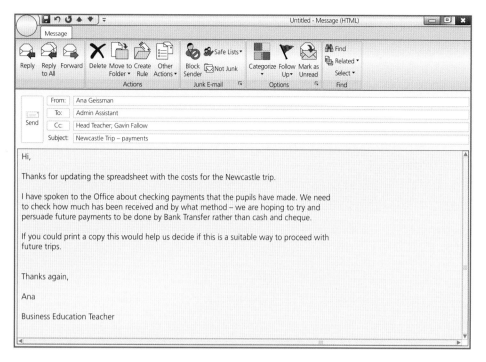

This is a continuation of the spreadsheet task.

This task is testing your ability to consolidate data using the most appropriate method.

How to!

In this instance the most effective (and quickest) method is by Creating (i.e. Insert Ribbon > Pivot Table) a Pivot table. So that it makes sense (SQA call this 'fit for purpose') it is a good idea to rename the headings – Sum of, Column labels and Row labels are not really 'fit for purpose'.

- Drag the Transaction field to the section Report filter.
- Drag the Method field to the section Column labels (the main point of the Pivot table).
- Drag the Trip ID field to the section Row labels (there are four Trips).
- Finally, drag the Amount field to the section Σ Values.

Below shows the Design View for the Pivot table – takes about 5 minutes to do AND edit – honest – just go for it!

> **Note**
>
> Consolidated data can take the form of a Graph/Chart OR Subtotals/Outlining OR a Pivot table.

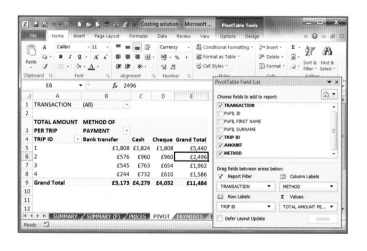

Make the following changes to the table:

Cell	Default	Change to
A3	Sum of AMOUNT	TOTAL AMOUNT PER TRIP, and
		Wrap Text in cell
B3	Column Labels	METHOD OF PAYMENT, and
		Wrap Text in cell
A4	Row labels	TRIP ID
Σ Values TOTAL AMOUNT PE…..		Double-click on this area and from Number Format option, choose currency, 0 decimal places
Printing		You need to revisit Page Layout to put on gridlines, your name, etc.

END OF FINAL IT ASSIGNMENT TASK

Additional task

This database task has been included to cover the skill of adding an aggregate which is NOT included in the Report Wizard.

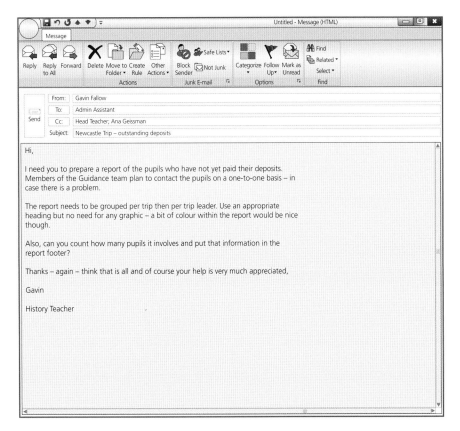

This task is testing your ability to search a database by creating a Query using very simple criteria. It is also testing your skills in creating grouping and inserting formula (not available in the summary options in the Report Wizard) in DB reports.

How to!

The first part of this task requires you to Create a Query from more than one table. The criteria you need to apply is very simply **Yes** for Team Leader and **No** for Deposit Paid. However, three tables are required for this query because the information needed for the report is stored in three different tables – Trip Details, Pupil Details and Teacher Details.

- From the Create Ribbon, select Create Query and select the fields as shown in Design View. Key-in the Yes and No criteria as appropriate.

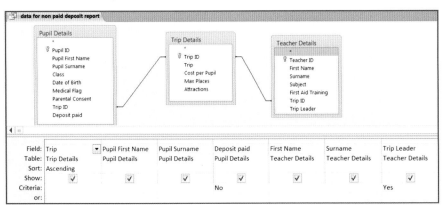

- Save the query using a memorable name that will help when creating the report.
- Select Report Wizard from the Create Ribbon.
- Select all fields in the query (except Deposit paid and Trip Leader) in the following order – Trip, First Name, Surname, Pupil First Name, Pupil Surname.
- Grouping should be done by Trip and then by Surname (of the Teacher not the Pupil).
- Choose landscape as there are only seven records to be displayed – it will be easier to edit under time pressure.

Once you have created the report, you can make adjustments in Design View – mainly:

1 Make the Report Header **bold**, **black** to make it stand out.
2 Delete the First Name label and rename the surname label – Trip Leader – in the Page Header section.
3 Move the First Name detail box in front of surname in the Trip Header section.
4 Delete the Pupil Surname label and Rename the Pupil Surname label – Pupil Name – in the Page Header section.
5 Move the Pupil Surname label to overlap the Pupil First Name – it looks nicer.
6 Use the **a b|** option in the Design controls and place in report footer.
7 In the text box, key-in a suitable label Number of Pupils.
8 In the Unbound box, key-in =**Count**([Surname]).

Hints & tips

*Make sure you know the difference between the label **Aa** and text box **ab|** function in Report Footers and Report Page Footers.*

Remember

The formula needs a bracket before and after the ([Field name]).

The design view should look something like this:

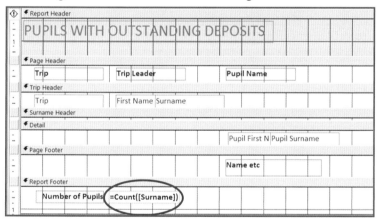

and the finished report like this:

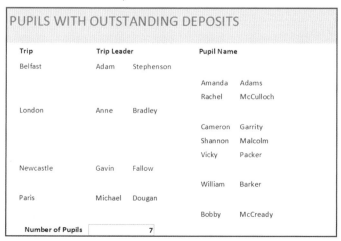

149

Appendices

Appendix 1
Understanding standards

Spreadsheet
Make sure your name is on every printout.
Make sure you have applied gridlines and/or row and column headings as specified.
Make sure ALL formulae and values are VISIBLE. ● Make sure you use the most appropriate formula. ● Addition of a range of more than two cells – always use SUM. ● Only use + sign when adding two cells or more than two non-adjacent cells. ● For subtractions never use =SUM at the start of the formula. ● IF statements must contain both conditions – THEN and ELSE, e.g. IF(something, then, else).

Database
Make sure your name is on every printout – print any tables and queries (export) using word processing – this allows you to put your name and any other information in the footer. It also means that all data is visible.
Make sure you know the difference between a form/report footer and a page footer – Your name, etc. should ALWAYS be in the page footer – never the form/report footer.
Make sure ALL data in a Form or Report is VISIBLE – this can only be done in DESIGN view.

Word processing
Make sure your name is on every printout – in the footer or header regardless of what else is specified for the footer or header.
Use a consistent date format within a document (unless otherwise stated). ● 0 Month 0000 ● 0th Month 0000 ● 0/0/00 ● 00/00/0000
Never use 'the' in a date.
Graphics should NEVER be clipped by a margin or cover any text.
Capitals should be used consistently throughout a document, for example: ● At the start of a sentence. ● For proper nouns, for example, names.

Word processing
Headings should be enhanced in some way, for example: ● block capitals (with or without bold) ● initial capitals with bold ● initial capitals with underline ● increased font size (with or without bold) ● headings with initial capitals for example, Appointments in January – the small words should not have a capital letter as shown.
Always be consistent with punctuation, for example: ● one or two (consistent) spaces at the end of a sentence ● one space after commas, colons, semi-colons, brackets ● hyphen has no spaces, a dash has a space before and after ● abbreviations do not need a full stop ● numbered items do not need a full stop ● bullets should be left aligned unless otherwise stated and line spacing, for example: ● two line spaces after a paragraph ● two line spaces between items in a letter ref, date, address, salutation and complimentary close ● at least four line spaces between the complimentary close and name/designation ● at least two spaces between the designation and enc.

Adapted from sources available on SQA's website.

Solution to calculated fields

Task	Calculation required = using proper syntax	
Class Fee to be reduced by 10%	[Class Fee]*0.9	(the use of 0 is optional)
Class Fee to be reduced by 2.5%	[Class Fee]*0.975	(try and think 1.000 – 0.025) or 97.5%
Class Fee to be reduced by 12.5%	[Class Fee]*0.875	(this is the same as 1.000 – 0.125) or 87.5%
Class Fee to be increased by 10%	[Class Fee]*1.1	(this is the same as 110% i.e. 100% + 10%)
Class Fee to be increased by 2.5%	[Class Fee]*1.025	(this is the same as 102.5% i.e. 100% + 2.5%)
Class Fee to be increased by 12.5%	[Class Fee]*1.125	(this is the same as 112.5% i.e. 100% + 12.5%)
Price to be increased by 15%	[Price]*1.15	(this is the same as 115% i.e. 100% + 15%)
Discount of 15% due on Amount Owing	[Amount Owing]*0.15	(this is the same as 15%)

How to create a large document

WP File – Large document practice

Create the following document as shown:

Key-in an equals sign followed by rand(10,10) as shown – this will generate random text for practising the basics – 10 paragraphs of 10 sentences of random text.

```
=rand(10,10)
```

The document should be about three pages long. Split the paragraphs as follows:

- At the top of the document key-in – First Section.
- At the top of the third paragraph key-in – Second Section.
- At the top of the second paragraph in this section, key-in the following tabulated text – set the tab stop at 3 cm on the Ruler.

ID Number	Name
00234	Anne Bradley
00245	Lauren Dougan
00256	Calum MacDonald
00267	Adam Stephenson

At the top of the third paragraph in this section, key-in the following small table as shown.

- At the top of the next paragraph key-in – Third Section.
- In the middle of the second paragraph of this section key-in the following table – remove gridlines.

Part 1	Introduction
Part 2	Development
Part 3	Results
Part 4	Conclusion
Part 5	References

Weekly Staff Rota	Monday	Tuesday	Wednesday	Thursday	Friday	Saturday
Staff 1						
Staff 2						
Staff 3						
Staff 4						
Staff 5						
Staff 6						
Staff 7						
Staff 8						

- At the top of the last paragraph key-in – Final Section.
- Save with the filename Large document practice.

Almost all manuscript correction signs (or proofreading symbols) follow the same pattern. There is a mark in the margin (left or right margin) along with specific information about the changes that should be made. A mark will also be made in the text where the correction has to be made.

Sign in Margin[1]	Example As shown on the document	What it means
UC or CAPS	an aqua thon	Change the underlined letter a to a Capital letter (upper case) … an Aquathon
lc	Yours Faithfully	Change the underlined letter F to a small letter (lower case) Yours faithfully
u/s	Computers	Apply underline to Computers – the underlined word Computers
bold	Select the control key.	Change the underlined word control to bold format … Select the **control** key.
italics	as appropriate	Change the underlined words as appropriate to italic format … *as appropriate* …
◯	We c an help	Remove the space between the word to read: We can help
N.P.	competition. The race results	Create a new paragraph at the place indicated (Hint – press enter twice) …………………….. competition. The race results …
run on	for your final afternoon. Please advise	Join 2 paragraphs into one … for your final afternoon. Please advise
ठ	as in the previous years.	Delete the scored out word the as indicated … as in previous years.
ʌconstantly	are ʌ trying to improve	Insert the word constantly at the place indicated … are constantly trying to improve
TRS	commitment and efforts.	Change the order of the words as indicated (horizontally) … efforts and commitment.

trs	↱ English ↱ Administration ↰	Change the order of the words as indicated (vertically) Administration English
	(Change margins to 2·54 cm (1 inch))	Follow the instructions[2] within the circle – do not key-in the words in the circle – use PageSetup to change margins.
stet	we are ~~delighted~~ *~~happy~~*	Keep the cancelled word delighted indicated by the dotted line[3] ... we are delighted ...
In full	bed <u>&</u> breakfast	Change the underlined abbreviation & to the full meaning ... bed and breakfast
(Interruption)	Unclear or unusual word is normally underlined	This is used when a word is unclear/unusual and it is most commonly used to confirm the spelling ... interruption.

(1) A correction made in the document usually has a corresponding mark in the margin – otherwise it could be easily missed when corrections are being made.

(2) Where instructions are written in the margin or at the end of a document, they are usually placed in a circle to show that they are not to be keyed-in/printed.

(3) **Stet (means – let it stand)** – when the new and original words have **both** been crossed out, key-in the word with the dotted line underneath.

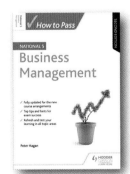  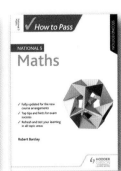